Mental Health Fight of The Heroes In Blue

How to Mentally Survive Working As A Police Officer

Scott Medlin

Foreword

Although we come from different generations, I believe that Officer Scott Medlin and I share many of the same beliefs and life experiences, from our patriotism, our faith, to our calling to the profession of law enforcement, and, most importantly, our love of and dedication to our family. When my friend and colleague Scott asked me to write the Foreword to his book, I was both overwhelmed and hesitant, as this is such an important subject which is not always easy to discuss, especially in the profession of law enforcement, where we are exposed to things and situations the human brain is not designed to comprehend.

We are exposed to the worst of the human condition, expected to magically fix the situation, and then move on to the next call. If what we experienced affects us emotionally, spiritually, or physically, we are expected to "suck it up" and get over it. When we do this long enough, year after year, with no outlet, emotions begin to overload and look for an outlet or release valve. That outlet can be either a positive one that brings healing or a negative one, which brings destruction.

Scott has selflessly served our country as a United States Marine. Now he serves his community as a police officer, and he is one of the best I have seen – that guy that you want as your backup when everything is going sideways. Throughout his career, he has experienced numerous situations that have taken their toll on him, just as they have on countless other police professionals. I am so proud of my friend for having the courage to address and tackle the subject of PTSD and mental health concerns in the law enforcement profession.

The statistics are overwhelming. When we think of the dangers of law enforcement, we typically think of the number of officers killed in the line of duty, and they are staggering. According to the Officer Down Memorial Page (ODMP), 146 officers were killed in the line of duty in the United States in 2019. Already as of the first quarter of 2020, 28 officers have been killed. These numbers are unacceptable. Even more disturbing, however, is that 228 officers committed suicide in 2019, and at least 50 have taken their own lives in the first quarter of 2020 – even more unacceptable.

I have served in the profession of law enforcement for over 30 years. I have seen and experienced many things that have taken their toll on me, but somehow, I seem to have come out of that career relatively unscathed. Ironically, however, shortly after Scott asked me to write this Foreword, I was involved in a freak accident which left me paralyzed from the neck down. Because of my faith and my amazing doctors, nurses, and therapists, I have miraculously begun to recover the use of my limbs. I am now able to walk on my own. This experience, though, has played games with my psyche. How did I survive three decades in the law enforcement profession and end up like this in my retirement? I am old enough and humble enough now, to know that I must find that positive outlet or release valve to deal with this, which will lead me to healing.

It is my hope and prayer that you were drawn to this book because you, too, are looking for that positive way of dealing with PTSD or whichever other challenges you may be facing. Or perhaps you know someone who is dealing with these challenges, and you are looking for a way to help. Do the most courageous thing you can do – have a challenging conversation and use this book as a tool to guide you. Through the years, several of my law enforcement friends have taken their own lives. These situations overwhelmed me, and I questioned myself as to why I did not see any obvious signs of trouble. Perhaps if I was armed with the information in Scott's book, I might have been able to intervene and make a difference.

Scott has the courage to address one of the most challenging aspects of our profession, and one of the least talked about. I implore you to channel Scott's courage to help yourself or someone you know.

Phil Carlson
Orange County Sheriff's Office, Orlando, FL, (Ret.)
U.S. Dept. of Homeland Security – FLETC (Ret.)

Table of Contents

Introduction

It is much more exciting (and in the case of Hollywood, *fruitful*) to depict the men and women in blue as legendary, stoic warriors who know neither fear nor hesitation. You have seen the shows and movies.

Reality, however, favors another interpretation – a much more humane one. In recent years especially, the world has seen just how humane police officers really are. They can make mistakes, feel pain, and even engage in self-harming behaviors.

In fact, officer suicides have exceeded the number of officers killed in the line of duty. Just like all other suicides, each one brings with it massive collateral damage for the loved ones, friends, and community of the officer.

These grim statistics are discussed to not to ruin your day, but to shed light on an issue that desperately needs it. The purpose of this book is to explore the challenges that come along with the mental fight in policing.

I will share a variety of strategies and treatment options from my own journey. I have also recruited the help of a doctor specializing in neuro-linguistic programming, a psychologist, and a life coach, to really dig into the nuances of the mental-health side of policing.

This book is not intended to read like a technical manual, because that will not help you apply these concepts. I am going to share my experiences in law enforcement as well, so you can marry the ideas with real-world applications.

Of the many adversaries that I have faced throughout my law enforcement career, the mental fight has been the toughest. To outsiders, the end of a shift appears to be a time to relax. Even though you have walked out of the "line of fire," various stressors may still preoccupy your mind.

While I am not a licensed psychiatrist, doctor, or clinical expert, I have spent twelve short years in law enforcement. During that time, I just about covered the spectrum when it comes to challenging and frequently plain' ole unpleasant experiences.

As a result of this career and two deployments to Iraq, I have suffered from a number of mental health issues throughout various points in my life, including post-traumatic stress disorder (PTSD), anxiety, depression, addictions, mood swings, and becoming physically ill due to stress.

You might be thinking, "Wow, this guy does not know how to get help himself, let alone guide others." Well, the thing is, I did get the help, and I will continue to work on my mindset and wellness. You should do the same. The fact that I am still affected to a degree by these issues brings me to two critical points that I hope you will carry with you throughout this book and beyond.

First and foremost, the most crucial distinction separating mental illness from physical illness involves *healing time*. A sprained ankle will go away after a few weeks of physical therapy. In contrast, you will need to continue practicing self-care and mindfulness to maintain your mental health, after overcoming the worst of a mental illness.

I hope that my experiences and the insights provided in this book from clinical experts will help you realize that you have a support system. Like you, I have experienced mental setbacks and stressful occurrences due to policing. I hope this book provides you with insight that other learning experiences cannot.

Make sense? As convenient as it may seem, we cannot conceptualize mental illness as rationally as other more mechanical issues. It is not a matter of "identify the problem, get the tools you need, solve it, and never worry about it again." It is an ongoing process.

This process cannot begin, of course, if you do not first acknowledge the problem. It may very well be true that you are not as profoundly affected as some of your peers. Still, if you are in law enforcement or a similarly stressful field, you are definitely at risk of a *mental battle*.

We know this, not only because of the statistic mentioned earlier but because of the many other (*non-suicidal*) manifestations of stress that law enforcement professionals and their loved ones' experience.

Few would argue that this problem does indeed exist. However, the real struggle is getting people to come together to address the mental fight in law enforcement as it is an uncomfortable topic. Neither the affected nor those around them want to talk about it. This crumbling standard, however, is unacceptable. It is the impetus for this book.

Through a comprehensive review of the data, the physiology of stress and depression, and the leading strategies used to lower suicide and self-harm risk, this book will attack this problem from a multitude of angles.

You will be introduced to a lot of specific information and even if you cannot remember all of it, just compare it to a food buffet. You might not be able to consume everything, but you will still get plenty. The more you can consume, the better, but do not get sick.

I understand some of this information will be confusing, but the more you can learn, the better you will be at identifying issues. Just when you are about to give up on reading the terminology, I will present the uplifting solutions. I'll explain more about that in a bit.

So let us begin with comprehending the battle we are up against, and can overcome.

Understanding the Mental Fight in Policing

Before we dive in, I would like to give you a snapshot of just what the mental fight looks like in the context of policing in 2020 and beyond.

First and foremost, we need to define the landscape by sweeping through the most indicative statistics. A review of the landscape and how real this problem is will give you context while stressing the importance of caring for your mental wellbeing. Even if you do not feel affected by suicidal thoughts at this point, it is crucial to learn how you can prevent future suicidal ideations.

For example, would you ever think that a police officer may be at increased risk for drug addiction and abuse? It seems highly counterintuitive, right? Especially for officers who spend a significant portion of their time dealing with violent, erratically behaving addicts.

Did you know that law enforcement officers also abuse alcohol and substances? In fact, the rates are disproportionately elevated due to the occupational stressors. Even though officers frequently see how terrible the drugs are, highly stressed officers may not be deterred if they do not have the necessary mental health tools.

The only way to create change is by coming together as a community and engaging in fascinating discussions. In this book, I will illuminate how the mind works. We will focus on how the brain processes stressful stimuli, and how we can train it to better handle negativity. This is part of the "theory" component of this book, and I really want you to have a balanced sense of its importance. I am not training you to become endocrinologists, because I myself am very far from that level of knowledge. So do not be stressed if you quickly forget that RAS stands for *reticular activating system*.

What is more important is that you can internalize the *ideas* that these fancy words represent so you can apply them more readily and practically. We will discuss how you can filter out negativity and address harmful thought patterns.

Next, we are going to explore a slightly less traveled road: the effect of the body on the mind. We all know that the brain is so powerful that it can do crazy things to our bodies, including making us actually feel pain when there is no physical basis for it (*crazy, right?*). But have you come to appreciate the effect that the body has on the mind? Sure, the body does not have all the fancy processing power that the brain does, but it still sends data back to the brain.

For example, if you ate junk for a week and exercised for less than 30 minutes, you would not feel very motivated. You may even engage in negative thought patterns. All of this is highly relevant for law enforcement officers, so we are going to cover this topic in depth.

By understanding how both the body and the mind affect your mental health and wellbeing, you will be better equipped to identify the signs and symptoms of suicide risk. To that end, we have dedicated a significant chapter to this concept.

Yes, we leave the diagnosis to doctors, but how can they make one if you never call to schedule an appointment because you did not recognize the signs and symptoms? You are responsible for seeking support from a doctor, who can then help you understand, diagnose, and treat the underlying problems.

As such, it is highly prudent that you are at least given an overall tour of the finer points of depression, PTSD, anxiety disorders, substance abuse, and the other issues that contribute to self-harm and suicide. We can all recognize the more straightforward symptoms, but much of this chapter could very well surprise you!

Finally, we are going to divvy up the solution to this pressing problem of officer suicide into two parts: strategies and treatments. As implied, the strategies chapter will focus on methods you can follow outside the doctor's office to improve the sustainability of your mental health throughout your career. Treatments will focus on the methods that professionals use to directly treat PTSD, stress, anxiety, depression, and so on.

The very last note I will add before we proceed to the first chapter is a bit of a disclaimer. I will be fairly blunt throughout this book, but please do not take offense to my result-driven approach. This book is focused on you, and I want you to know that you are never alone.

So why the bluntness, you ask? Because this takes work and involves acceptance of a realization that we may have been trying to deny. Overcoming and/or preventing mental illness is work, especially when you must put on that uniform every day and venture into some of the darkest places.

It is okay to be vulnerable. It is okay to feel overwhelmed as long as you do not feel sorry for yourself. If you enter that malingering mentality, you will find it harder to dig yourself out.

If you commit yourself to working on your issues, instead of falling into the self-pity trap, you will surely win the battle with a more vigorous defense system. Just like an athlete, it takes discipline to get there. You will have to do things you might not feel like doing.

It is my great honor to present you with this book in hopes that you can extract even one useful lesson from it. That being said, let us look away from this issue no longer as we address the mental fight in policing.

Chapter I: The Numbers

Simply being told that the number of officer suicides has exceeded that of officers lost in the line of duty does not provide the entire picture. To keep up with our *"going to the doctor"* metaphor, it is merely an overall prognosis.

If all you said when reporting to the doctor was, "I feel sad," the doctor would not just take that as gospel and whip out the prescription pad – especially nowadays.

No, they would try to capture as many data points as they could to identify *exactly* what the problem is.

When do you feel the saddest?

On a scale of 1-10, how would you rate your sadness?

How your sadness affected your relationships and quality of life?

When did your sadness start, and has it worsened?

How is your health and wellbeing otherwise?

What do you do for work?

And so on. The point is this: As boring as it may sound on the surface, a smartly assembled set of statistics can provide hugely helpful insights that go way beyond merely stating that there is a problem.

I am sharing this with you for two reasons. First, I hope you will clearly understand that this is not a "doom and gloom" kind of book. Yes, we are obviously going to cover some pretty somber issues. But, by bringing these topics into the limelight, we will identify appropriate solutions.

Lastly, the more causal factors you can piece together, the more targeted your solution can be. If you never admit your twinkie obsession to your trainer, and you do not work to fix it, that treadmill is not going to help that much. Similarly, if you do not accept support from healthcare professionals to help you overcome your mental health battle, you will continue to struggle.

Enough metaphors - it is time to get to the statistics. Do me a favor: Please do not just breeze through these. I do not expect you to memorize the actual numbers. However, you absolutely should remember and appreciate the causal factors that these statistics represent.

Post-Traumatic Stress Disorder (PTSD)

We are going to cover symptoms of stress-related disorders in a later chapter. For now, it is essential to know that Post-Traumatic Stress Disorder (PTSD) is an issue that many police officers combat. According to a US Department of Justice report, 15 percent of police officers exhibit symptomology consistent with PTSD. You are not alone if you experience PTSD.

15 percent is way more significant than it sounds, especially for larger departments. For example, imagine if you have 2,000 officers in your department, more than 300 of them would be statistically likely to display PTSD symptoms.

When most of us think of PTSD, we think of Marines and soldiers returning from deployment in active combat zones. While this is a huge problem that is thankfully receiving more and more attention, the image needs to be expanded to include law enforcement officials. We need to work together to take down barriers, reduce stigma, and help our fellow heroes not feel insecure about reporting their symptoms and seeking support.

Another consideration I want to emphasize involves the nature of the trauma. Violence, whether the officer witnesses the aftermath, or participates in it themselves, is not the only form of trauma that can cause PTSD.

In my twelve years in law enforcement and two deployments for Operation Iraqi Freedom, I have seen plenty of violence. However, I know that the biggest fight is mental and emotional, and the mind can experience trauma in many ways.

Just consider a few of the everyday experiences that contribute to PTSD among law enforcement professionals.:

- Seeing someone hurt themselves.

- Arriving first to the scene of a drug overdose.

- Informing loved ones that the person has been hurt or killed.

- Helping someone who has been a victim of abuse.

In fact, on the first call that left me feeling traumatized, the only violence I saw was self-inflicted. A person had severely hurt themselves, and I had to listen to the phone call when loved ones were notified. I will never get that image out of my head, though many grislier images have followed.

A strong trigger for many of us, police or not, is child victimization. Whether it is abuse of some kind or worse, these horrific crimes can very easily cause PTSD after just one incident.

Addiction (Substances)

The actual science, the *neurophysiology* of addiction, has taught us some fascinating things about addiction that defy the conventional understanding.

Still, the correlation between trauma and addiction is not going anywhere soon. It is unanimously agreed upon. In fact, traumatization is a reliable indicator of future drug abuse.

Police are unfortunately positioned at the end of a downward spiral on this one. As logic dictates, child abuse and rape victims, military veterans with PTSD, and other populations at greater risk for drug abuse tend to perpetrate crimes at a higher rate than non-drug-abusers.

Police respond to these crimes, and are in turn, are traumatized by some of the violent, perverse, and otherwise awful things that they see. This, in turn, makes them more likely to become drug abusers.

It seems crazy, right? Police officers have a front-row seat to the worst movie in history by watching drug addicts ruin their own lives. So, why on Earth would police turn around and abuse alcohol and other substances?

The reality is that the trauma is simply too intense of a motivator, and drugs are an "attractive" option when someone is seeking an escape.

Think of it as a chemical reaction. Yes, sorry, we are revisiting chemistry class for a moment. Remember catalysts? Basically, a *catalyst* is an element that is used to provide enough energy for a chemical reaction to occur.

Your brain is the experiment, and overcoming trauma is the chemical reaction. While many civilians can overcome the energy threshold on their own, experiencing trauma repeatedly raises that threshold significantly for law enforcement and military personnel.

In order to avoid more blatant forms of self-harm, some officers use drugs and alcohol to cope, even though it is a crappy coping mechanism. Our aim here is to replace that coping mechanism with a much healthier and more sustainable one.

Think this is just a couple of men and women per department? Think again.

According to Psychology Today, a staggering 25 percent of police officers *"on the street"* experience substance abuse issues, whether it is drugs or alcohol.

To provide some additional context, compare that 25 percent of police officers against less than 10 percent in the general population.

This report was published in 2018, and the numbers have probably not improved since then for several reasons. First, police are always held to a higher standard because of the string of highly controversial incidents that have taken place over the past decade.

It is excellent that the need for accountability is increasing, but that means police are under even greater scrutiny. Policies are more restrictive. Technology is entering the equation as we now use body cameras, are recorded by the general public, and are frequently bothered by the media.

Without a doubt, there have been a few bad apples that have soured things for the rest of us. Now, even a completely warranted and by-the-book use of force has a chance to spark riots, media outrage, suspensions, lawsuits, or even dismissal. With social media, news can quickly spread to thousands, mobilize passionate riots, and destroy reputations.

Now, you may be thinking, "Phew, glad I dodged the bullet on the whole addiction thing. I am not addicted to pain pills, alcohol, tobacco, porn, or anything else like that."

It is not to rain on your parade that I say this, but we need to keep you vigilant of your mindset. You may not be addicted to one of the usual suspects, but you could be locked into a negative mentality. For our purposes, that absolutely counts as an addiction, and I can prove it.

Addiction (Negative Mindset)

Most of us do not like to talk about it, especially since we think we are alone. Whether you are a police officer or a soldier who has seen action, or a totally "green" civilian who has had a very peaceful life, the ugly, violent and super weird thoughts may creep into your head just the same.

The thoughts tell us that we are not good enough. They encourage us to hurt *person x* and that *person y* is an […insert tasteless language…].

Is it a relief to hear that you are not the only one who has these thoughts? Did you know that psychologists have been chipping away at this issue for a few decades?

Psychologist Eric Klinger conducted a study in which participants recorded 500 of their thoughts at random times throughout the day. It was found that almost 20 percent of these thoughts were morbidly violent, ignorant, mean, perverse, and harmful. The weirdest part was the participants were everyday people, not extremists of any kind.

Some theorize that these types of thoughts once served a vital purpose because people from other tribes really would try to kill you. So, we are equipped with defensive thoughts due to evolution based on the survival of the fittest.

Wherever these thoughts come from, we have the power to bolster (or suppress) these ideations. In the case of police, the battle is an uphill one which is conflicted with many environmental and internal factors.

As police officers, we always see people at their worst. We are frequently lied to and manipulated. We experience heavy scrutiny, yet at the same time, supervisors and politicians can expect a lot of us.

All of these elements have proven themselves to be a dangerous cocktail with the nurturing of these dark thoughts. Most civilians can manage these thoughts with less difficulty. Still, even they often unhealthily air these thoughts out over a drink or seven.

In contrast, police officers may not have the luxury of distancing themselves from the dark underbelly of society. These police officers may become enslaved to these negative thoughts that affect every aspect of life. These negative mentalities can be manifested in several harmful ways, including problems with marital relationships, such as affairs or divorces.

The Good News

Alright, alright, you might be thinking – enough of the doom and gloom. Fair enough. This is the perfect junction to roll out the silver lining, so let us do just that.

The same mysterious, powerful, and mostly unexplored engine that drives addiction, PTSD, and negative mentalities can be used as a weapon against these problems. You just need to know how to properly leverage your powerful brain.

Did you know that there are yogis who have undergone tumor excisions, root canals, and other painful procedures and surgeries without a drop of anesthesia? With a little direction and plenty of discipline, the brain can do astoundingly amazing things.

The first step is to stop buying into the perception that your resolve is untouchable, just because you are a police officer. It is not. You are not. Bravery does not even really exist when you think about it.

You are not a "brave" person, or a "good" person, or any kind of "one-word" person. You are a person. You can and will do good and bad things. Why is it so crucial that you start with this? Because it detaches you from the need to fit into a societally structured mold. It allows you to make mistakes without hating yourself because you do not fit that mold.

So, we are leveraging the mightiness of this super-powered organ to help combat the stressful and sometimes traumatic nature of our jobs, as we will discuss in Chapter II.

We need to begin by accepting that we are mortal and fallible human beings. The next step is to learn how the brain filters and processes stimuli from the world around us. Sure, many mental illnesses have a hereditary component. However, that does not mean they cannot be heavily mediated by your active and consistent participation in the methods we will discuss.

When you understand how and why these negative thoughts and behaviors are coming about, you demystify the problem. This understanding adds a logical legitimacy to the issue, so you do not feel like you are just crazy or that it is just "the way it is."

That said, let me introduce our next chapter: **How the Mind Works**. I am not interested in (*or capable of*) providing you with a winding dissertation about the inner workings of the mind. What I am interested in, however, is identifying the key players that encourage depression, PTSD, and the other conditions that contribute to suicidal ideations and behaviors.

We have defined the landscape by showing you the numbers and talking a little bit about the specific mental health issues police officers must fight against. We are now going to delve into the "how." What happens between seeing the stimuli and developing the mental health issue? Get ready to explore the never-ending, but fascinating weirdness of the brain.

But before we take a deeper dive, let me start you on your first call to action.

That's right, before each chapter from here on out, I challenge you to take these specific actions (along with the strategies and treatments explained later in the book) to help your mindset.

CTA 1:

Write down five things you are grateful for. Use your pocket notepad if you have to. Do this as many times as you would like during the day, for the rest of your life.

Chapter II: How the Mind Works

Perhaps it is a little ambitious to phrase it this way. Let us say we are going to learn about how the mind interprets stimuli (in our case, trauma). Why is this relevant to a book about decreasing suicide risk throughout the law enforcement community? The answer leans heavily on the weird and cool science of perception.

This is not a psychology course, nor do I mean to get all Dalai Lama on you. But the "ingredient" that determines whether or not a person becomes depressed or addicted is not found in the stressful stimulus itself but within the person. Indulge me for just a moment, if you would.

Have you ever watched a documentary or news feature about a traumatic event? Let us say the Titanic, for example.

In the instance of the Titanic, it is fair to say that every one of the survivors went through a similarly traumatic ordeal. They were all on the ship, so they all had to do crazy and desperate things to survive.

If you were to interview the survivors, you would likely see that they exist on a vast spectrum of differing responses. Some embrace optimism and gratitude, while others have feelings of extreme guilt or depression.

Why?

They all went through the same ordeal, and yet, some of them were able to perceive the situation more positively than others. The only logical conclusion, then, that explains the difference in responses is that some had worked on their ability to cope, while others were not so well-equipped. We can view the world through a variety of lenses, and the perspective that we choose is up to us. This is a glass-half-full or half-empty situation.

This is the secret sauce we should be striving to create. Harnessing the mind's ability to cope and systematizing it should be our goal as law enforcement professionals.

However, training might be lackluster in this department, would you agree? Sure, the elevated incidence of depression and addiction among officers may be mentioned. You will likely have access to counseling after discharging your firearm in the line of duty, but what about preparation? What about before?

It is of little surprise to me that law enforcement training has yet to fully embrace the neuropsychology behind depression and suicide. I feel that it is a very, very nuanced and technical topic that involves one of the most insanely complex mysteries around.

Yes, I am talking about the brain. As stated more eloquently in Robin Rosenberg's *Fundamentals of Psychology: The Brain, The Person, The World,* a whole lot is going on up there. We have 100 billion neurons to try to keep track of, in fact.

Each of these neurons, also known as brain cells, has the potential to store and transmit information. A typical example that illuminates both a critical function of these neurons and their relationship with the body is the "hand on the hot stove" situation.

A kid puts their hand on a hot stove. Within milliseconds, an "arc" occurs. The pain signal travels from the hand's nerve receptors to the command center in the brain. The hand is asking the brain, "It is really hot, and this hurts, what the heck do I do? You are the smart one!"

Of course, the brain says, "Abort! Abort! Get out of there!" In doing so, the neurons in the pain center of the brain quickly send a signal back to the hand and arm, telling it to pull away immediately.

Why the neurology lecture, you might ask? Because you need to understand the fundamentals of how the brain communicates with itself and the body if you hope to gain control over your own mental health. If you cannot speak the language, how will you get anything done?

In order to really learn that language, we will need to take a closer look at how the mind perceives, filters, and processes the stimuli around it. As mentioned, perception is an integral part of this equation, and it is the first gear to turn, so let us start with perception.

The Reticular Activating System

This section is not directly focused on our purpose of addressing depression and suicide in the law enforcement community; however, it makes a very strong case for perception in terms of its influence over our mental wellbeing.

In Ed Mylett's *Maxout Your Life,* the author goes out of his way to describe what is known as the reticular activating system, or RAS. This fancy term refers to a small portion of the brain that serves a critical function: to determine whether we consciously acknowledge the stimuli around us.

Before we jump into this freakishly futuristic piece of brain-tech, I want to pose a question to you: why? Why would a high-performing entrepreneur like Ed Mylett, who has never been a neurologist, care about the reticular activating system?

Because he understands the power of positive thinking. As a highly accomplished person, he knows that negative thoughts can make the difference between achieving your goals and settling for a mediocre life.

This is easily ported to our context as law enforcement officials. A negative mindset can be much more harmful to a police officer for various reasons, and a positive mindset is instrumental to longevity in this career field. Now, what the heck is this RAS thing again? Why does RAS matter so much in terms of perception and mindset?

Well, essentially, the RAS is a filter. It is a complex network of neurons that determines which pieces of sensory information (except smell) are worthy of conscious appraisal and which should just be totally ignored.

Why is this necessary? Well, you might be thinking of "sensory information" as somebody telling you something or a song playing in the background. Still, to your brain, it can be much, much more discrete than that.

17

For example, a change in air pressure or temperature. The way you just shifted half a pound of additional weight onto the ball of your left foot. Think about the 27 hairs on your head that just shifted as you closed that door and caused a small gust of air.

Can you imagine the anxiety, no, the insanity we would have if we had no choice but to consciously register each one of these tiny details? The experts say, in fact, that our senses are exposed to a ridiculous *300* pieces of information *every second.*

That is absolutely nuts. What is even crazier is that the RAS actually "lets in" about 100 pieces of sensory input per second. When people say the brain is a "supercomputer," they are not kidding.

Alright, so fascination aside, let us consider the implications of RAS in our current context. We have this reticular activating system thing that filters information, but who tells it what to do? Where is the guy saying, "Okay, let this in, but not that, and only let this one in this time?"

This is where it gets a little dicey. If we could all just declare to ourselves, "Reticular activating system, you are only allowed to appraise awesome things consciously," we would all be super awesome and positive human beings. Boom. Done.

Life, however, from a biological and evolutionary standpoint, is not always awesome. Someone may try to hurt you physically. Someone may cheat on you. There may be emotional wounds. For goodness sake, you could trip and break your nose as you are trying to make an arrest.

For that reason, RAS has some hard and fast rules in terms of things that will always grab your attention, like a threat of physical harm, the mention of your name, and so on.

So, it is healthy to be *aware* of potentially harmful, negative things. We cannot train our brains not to respond to this kind of stimuli. Yet, we need to make the critical distinction between awareness and indulgence.

Repetition is a crucial factor here. The more you are immersed in a negative environment, the harder the RAS must fight to stay positive. So, it is more likely that you will give in and become negative as well. That is where healthy awareness of negativity becomes unhealthy indulgence in negativity.

I am just as guilty as the rest of us on this one. As a law enforcement professional, my mind is exposed to negativity daily. Now, I fancy myself a strong person, and I still believe that, but I am a human. I still cave into negativity at times and can become negative.

The worst part about negativity as you have likely heard before, negativity is extremely skilled at "sucking you in." What starts with prolonged exposure, as I just mentioned, can be fed by confirmation bias.

Consider this scenario, I am steeped in this negative environment, right? So, I wake up in a bad mood most days. I start my morning by complaining to a coworker about the new extra-duty assignment I have been assigned.

Then, I become even more angrier when someone flees from me in their vehicle and gets away. For the rest of the day, week, month, and however long, I have this negative mindset, everything negative that happens is expected, and everything positive that happens is a fluke.

That is how tricky your own mind can be – especially the reticular activating system. When you are focusing on a certain mindset, things that would typically warrant your attention can actually fall by the wayside.

For example, consider the last scare you had with your child. If you do not have a child, let us say a family pet. You are out somewhere, looking after the little one who is standing to your left. You turn your back for literally three seconds to talk to someone. You turn back around, and the child is gone.

Immediately, your brain snaps into "find this kid" mode. A lot of stuff is happening (your endocrine system lights up, pumping some adrenaline, etc.), and the RAS is included in that. You quickly scan the playground as your eyes dart from kid to kid, checking to see if they are yours.

Research has shown that half of those kids could have been wearing beer helmets and wedding dresses, and you would never have noticed. Your RAS can be calibrated to focus on a particular stimulus, meaning it must block out other things that would usually get through.

Lo and behold, the child is discovered, simply standing to your right.

And that was just a five-second scare. Can you imagine five years of looking for negativity? It is no wonder you run into miserable people at the grocery store – the mind is a fickle being.

So, now you understand how the information that we consciously perceive, which is a process that is *partially* in our control, can influence our overall mindset. I also hope you have picked up on the idea that repetition and severity of stimulus both influence this perception heavily.

Speaking of repetition and its influence on perception and mindset, police officers in this era have found themselves up against an omnipresent opponent that previous generations did not have to deal with as much: *technology*.

Now, I do not mean that police officers of two or three decades ago had no access to technology of any kind. I am saying that police officers of past generations were not always inundated with texts, emails, social media, and other stimuli that tax the brain even more.

All they had to worry about in the 70s and 80s was squawking dispatchers (just kidding, we love you). Seriously, though, the daily flood of emails, texts, and other media is a problem that the law enforcement community needs to address, and pronto.

It is easy to overlook email as a stressful element when you think about policing because the Hollywood motif drives images of car chases and drug busts into our minds. The reality is a different picture entirely.

If a mountain of emails is not enough to push that stress to new thresholds, then the multitasking in the field certainly will be.

Picture this very real scenario:

An officer is speaking on their cell phone with the victim of a fraud while they keep one ear on the radio to know where their other officers are. Meanwhile, they are answering the message their sergeant just sent asking what the serial number is on their flashlight. Just then, they realize that their body camera is on and has to be labeled. At that moment, they receive an email reminding them of the training requirements they need to fulfill to comply with state requirements.

Can you imagine the poor reticular activating system now?

Moreover, the constant bombardment of texts, emails, and especially social media notifications tinkers with your brain's pleasure center in a way that can really affect concentration and mindset. Some people refer to it as a "dopamine loop" or a "reward system." Whatever you want to call it, we all know the feeling. You get that notification, and your brain gives you a little shot of happy juice. Not the 80-proof kind, mind you, but the kind your own brain creates.

Essentially, you become addicted to notifications because your brain is trained to be flooded with small "shots" of dopamine at a really high frequency. Then, when you have to respond to a call, you "come down," which can make that stabbing or drug overdose even grimmer.

Next, we have the issue of FOMO. Many police officers often prefer to groom themselves as stoic and tough. However, that toughness does not mean they do not need other people. It does not mean they do not want to hang out at bars, go on vacations, and enjoy the people around them.

If you have not heard of FOMO, it stands for "fear of missing out." We all have that friend or two on social media who apparently does not work. Every day is a picture in a new country, and everything in their life seems to just slide into place. This makes you feel like crap.

Imagine you just got a half-eaten burger thrown at you by some junkie who you had to shoo away from a business property like a derelict cat. By the time you get back to your vehicle, all you want is to check your phone and relax for literally 45 seconds before the nonsense continues.

You pop open your Facebook and start scrolling. You see example after example of this perfect world traveler we just discussed, and you have a moment of weakness so profound that you almost break into tears.

It is not just FOMO. The constant comparing yourself to your "friends" drives insecurity, anxiety, and depression. The ironic part is that *we* are the ones who should be celebrated in such a way. Realizing this, you might as well add a bit of anger into that already nasty cocktail.

Finally, though this does not conclude the long list of ways in which technology messes with us by any stretch, there is the sleep issue. Neuroscientists are still taking their time with this one, as it is a relatively recent phenomenon. They do not want to speak without objective facts behind them, but it is strongly theorized that all those gadgets we use affect sleep.

Here is the long and short of it. There is a gland in our brain called the pineal gland that acts as our body's bedtime and alarm system. When it is dark, the gland says, "Alright, time to pack it in. You need sleep." It then produces chemicals that help you feel sleepy.

During the day, of course, it is not producing those chemicals, because that would interfere with your ability to process information, communicate, respond to stimuli, and so forth.

So, how does the pineal gland know when to secrete sleepy time chemicals and when to stay out of the way? Light.

And what is that iPad, phone, or laptop blasting you with until seventeen seconds before your head hits the pillow? Light. See the conundrum here?

Sleep is paramount for everyone, but it is very, very important for depression. So, let us take stock here. You have got a police officer who is already experiencing negative thought patterns. They are addicted to social media, stressed, and depressed.

The one solace they should have, *sleep*, is eluding them as well. As they scroll through social media and/or watching movies and shows, they ironically feel stress relief. And on and on the loop goes. Where does it start for most of us? The work environment.

Therefore, it is more important than ever to *consciously seek out* a positive environment while consciously avoiding adverse environments. Environmental influence is so powerful because it is self-sustaining. It will provide a consistent stimulus of a certain kind. If you were simply trying to think positively in a negative environment, you would be fighting a losing battle.

Thankfully, or not, if you do not address the following component, the brain has a few other mechanisms that can influence what kind of mindset the law enforcement official finds themselves in.

We have all heard about how we are "wired" in a certain way. I am not a huge fan of this term because it implies that there is absolutely nothing we can change, and that is not true. Still, beyond the RAS, our brains do come with some "factory settings" that we need to be aware of.

This marks our transition from perception to processing. We have now decided to let the information in, but what determines how we handle it? Factory settings, for one.

Factory Settings Are Also a Thing (part one, we are wired a certain way, part two, we can change that with neuroplasticity, etc.)

This point pops up in interesting and controversial places. Whenever somebody does something inconceivable to the rest of us, such as molestation or serial murder, it is human nature for us to try and make sense of it all.

Why? Why would a human being do such a thing?

Obviously, police are confronted with this question very often. Some of us have different answers. A significant amount of us adopt the mentality of, "It does not matter why, I just clean up the mess" because staring directly at this dark potential is terrifying.

Then come the news pundits and politicians after the fact. Let us say the issue in question is a particularly terrible case of child molestation. Every once in a while, guest speakers and hosts, especially on political shows, will get into this debate:

Person 1: "Clearly, this person (the molester) was treated like human garbage from day one, and they lashed out."

Person 2: "Are you crazy? People are abused and neglected all the time, and you do not see 99 percent of them doing what this person did. They are just evil."

Now, first of all, we are talking about suicidal depression in this book, not criminal behavior. Still, the issue of "nature versus nurture" is very much at play in our situation.

I do not mean to give a wishy-washy answer. Still, the truth is that both your experiences/perceptive capabilities, per above, *and* the way you were "wired" contribute to your overall mindset.

To make things even a little more confusing for you, these elements can kind of switch tendencies. For example, the more malleable and fleeting of the two, nurture, can actually create rigid and unchanging thought patterns if the environment is consistent enough.

Conversely, the natural component, which by implication is something that cannot be changed, actually can be changed with adequate training. You have heard researchers say, for example, that certain things can "rewire the brain."

Phew, this is going to be a logical maze, eh? No worries, I have laid this all out in a very straightforward way. Think of these "factory settings," as the way your brain has wired the other half of your mindset.

You are Not in Control

"Of course, I am in control," you say. "I can command my brain to do anything, and it will make my body do it."

Alright, I will concede that. Absolutely. Barring any serious neurological or psychological issues, we all have freewill control of our actions.

However, there is a script running in the background, silently. A very, very old set of impulses, reflexes, and instincts that once helped us to escape from hostile tribesmen, frickin' dire wolves, and extreme weather patterns.

Humans are not iPhones. We need more than 28 seconds between software updates (I mean, really, it is getting ridiculous). We may be awakened in our active consciousness, but I am talking about deep-seated, evolutionary stuff here.

Example time! I know it sounds ridiculous, but our bodies are *still* worried about the ice age. Why do you think we love fats, carbs, sugars, and starches so much? Because our brains are telling us, "Yeahhh, pack it on. We are going to survive!"

This whole idea of the "paleo" diet is laughable for this reason. If you put a bag of chips in front of a Neanderthal, he would choose it over the berries every single time.

Our brains and bodies are not wired to step into harm's way unless it is to save a family member. Our minds and bodies have literally two goals in life: survive through fat and reproduce. That is one aspect of our "wiring" that is so hard for police officers.

Why? Think about it. Despite Hollywood depictions, you and I know that a lot of the job involves sitting around. What do our primitive brains tell us to do while we are sitting around? Load up on sugary, fatty crap! This, in turn, affects our mindset. The sugar especially makes that whole dopamine loop thing from earlier even worse.

Then, out of frickin' nowhere, we get a call and must launch into survival mode because our lives are in some level of danger every single time we respond to a call. Powered by the sympathetic nervous system, our endocrine glands pump out those "fight-or-flight" hormones.

Is it mixed with sugar and empty carbs? Yikes.

Anyway, we are feeling all this stress, we get to the call, and we handle it. However, hormones are not like neurons. You cannot just flicker hormones on and off instantly. That adrenaline sticks around for a while. As soon as it goes down, we get another call.

This constant track-switching from fight-or-flight to humdrum is entirely based on how we are wired, and there is little we can do about it. While the adrenaline is pumping, we are not digesting food because blood is being shunted to our muscles and brain.

We are also wired for repetition, which makes sense. The neurophysiology behind this, sorry for the big word, is genuinely fascinating. Unfortunately, it can be quite problematic as well. I will explain how in just a moment. Let us first see how repetition affects the nervous system.

Let us take a professional basketball player. This person has dribbled a ball tens of thousands of times, right? The same goes for passing, shooting, pivoting, and all the other fundamentals.

Your brain wants to help your body become more efficient in reducing energy costs, the chance of injury, and improve the chances of "survival" and victory.

So, how does it help? When you repeatedly do something, the brain says to itself, "Wow, this must be really important stuff. Let me give those nerve fibers a boost." It adds this substance to the nerves called myelin, which makes them even faster. It is called myelination.

Basically, when you repeat something enough times, your brain can communicate with the muscles used in that activity even faster.

In two words, muscle memory. Now, you might be thinking, why would you train your body to respond quickly ever be potentially harmful for a police officer?

Two reasons. First and foremost, myelination can be a powerful bad habit generator. For example, if you always check your Facebook after closing your car door, your brain will group those movements into one action and actually *tell* you to check your phone every time you shut that door.

See what I mean by not having at least full control?

The second and much more dangerous scenario involves quick decision-making in the field. If we do not train for every hostile encounter with equal emphasis on every option (i.e., gun versus taser versus spray, etc.), it could spell trouble.

Many officers like to go to the gun range on their own time, which I am not arguing against by any means. However, if they have super-myelinated the "draw and shoot" pathway in their nervous system without working on their other, non-lethal options, there may be problems.

Tragically, a man was shot in 2019 by an officer who intended to reach for his taser. Again, we have less control than you think.

How did this happen? Though I will not presume to know the inner workings of a man I have never met, I immediately thought of myelination when I heard this story. Indeed, the word "muscle memory" was thrown around a lot in reference to this case.

The officer *told* his brain to reach for the taser, but unbeknownst to him, the officer's mind said, "I am going to do what you have trained me to do." In that adrenaline-filled situation, the brain will take the fastest and most familiar route to a solution, and that is what it did.

Also, the officer, in that case, was out of compliance for keeping the taser on the same hip as the gun, but you get the point.

The Difference Between "Oh Well" and Making a Change

So, let us recap for just a moment here. The brain has these "factory settings" that it uses in a mostly subconscious capacity to meet our oldest and most primitive survival needs. Stay warm, reproduce, fight, eat, etc.

27

As a concerned law enforcement community addressing the unacceptable issue of suicide in our own ranks, we need to learn how this primitive drive or "wiring" affects our mindset. The brain does not care about being "happy" in this sense, but merely staying alive.

What we need to do is reconcile these two objectives using targeted strategies and treatments that we will discuss in later chapters. For now, I just want you to appreciate the connection. We have examined it from three perspectives just now, so let us review:

1) Our survival drive tells us to sit still, stay out of danger, and eat crappy food. The crappy food, especially sugar, contributes to dopamine starvation and, subsequently, negative mentalities.

2) By jumping headfirst into danger, then relaxing, then doing it all again, we are causing our hardwired fight-or-flight system to pump hormones into our bodies that mess with vital functions and affect our mindset negatively.

3) Both our formal training (gun range, etc.) and our personal habits (phone use in the car) condition the brain to reinforce both good and bad habits.

I realize this is painting a pretty grim picture, but do not worry, I bring good news. As mentioned, you can actually fight each and every one of these symptoms. You cannot fundamentally change your will to survive, but you can mediate the effects it has on you.

Neuroplasticity! It is a thing.

Every few years, the word "neuroplasticity" pops up in advertisements for brain-training mobile applications, the Alzheimer's discussion, and a few other places. I mean, from a marketing perspective, it is kind of a gold mine. Neuroplasticity? That just sounds cool.

You have likely already heard about neuroplasticity through one of the avenues mentioned above, but if you have not, no worries. Allow me to give you a plain-speak rundown of what this phenomenon is and how we can take advantage of it in our particular context.

Think about the word – plastic. Something that is plastic is malleable, flexible. Your brain is far more flexible and adaptable than you think.

Sure, we form habits and clutter our minds with distractions that can impede the learning process. It really is harder to learn a language when you get older. It truly is tougher to teach an old dog new tricks.

The good news, however, is that you are never too old to take advantage of neuroplasticity. I recommend checking out the work of Dr. Joe Dispenza, renowned neurologist and author, who explains the concept perfectly.

In the words of Dr. Dispenza, "Neurons that fire together, wire together." As I detailed in the above section about myelination or muscle memory, the brain is all about identifying and fortifying neural pathways.

Let us dive into that concept a little more. Learning is a complex machine that I do not purport to understand fully. However, I do know that neuroplasticity is a central component to it. When you put in the time and effort it takes to listen to a mentor, read, watch a video, or however, else you learn, your brain takes notice.

Bob seeks out information regarding how he can qualify for the SWAT team. The brain says, "Oh, okay. Bob must really want to know how to get on the SWAT team." Watching someone else do it is just step one. This gives your brain an incomplete blueprint, a starting point. Actually, attempting the task is where neuroplasticity really shines.

So, Bob goes to the SWAT training sessions to observe, practices at the range, exercises, and studies SWAT tactics. When he finally makes the team, his first room entry during training is not bad at all, but it could improve. Actually, that is just what he does, through repetition. Each time, his room entry continues to improve.

How?

Well, each time Bob practiced, his brain was sending feelers out into that swirling and mysterious cloud of 100 billion neurons, trying to find the "path" that would enable Bob to become an effective SWAT operator.

Each time Bob made a mistake, his brain scratched off that part of the path, just like when you take the wrong turn in a maze, and you have to backtrack. Eventually, you find your way through.

Most of us without a background in neurology have an over-simplified understanding of how the brain learns new information and applies it. We picture the brain as this big, empty jar, and everything we have learned is just like a cookie in that jar.

As Dr. Dispenza explains, neuroplasticity, change, and learning are much more complicated. Each task we learn is represented by a pathway – a string of connected neurons that have been plucked from that cloud and given a specific function.

How is this relevant to our lives as law enforcement professionals? There is a whole set of significant implications that this immaculate ability of the brain introduces. Let us start with memory recall first.

Why Police Should Care About Neuroplasticity

How great is it to commiserate with old friends about the crazy stuff you did before you joined the police force (not after, of course)? When you think about the logic behind this, it is kind of crazy, actually.

What I mean is, when you remember something from your past in this way, you produce an emotional response with absolutely zero stimuli occurring around you. The neurologists, Dr. Dispenza, included, have some fascinating things to say about this.

When you are involved in any event, good or bad, all of your senses send data to your brain, which forms a unique pattern of neurons specific to that event. It sounds weird at first, but when else are you going to see, smell, hear, touch and/or taste the *exact* same thing twice?

So, think of your brain in this instance as a disposable camera. The event occurs, your senses quickly process the information, and an imprint is left on your mind in the form of a highly specific clumping of neurons. That is like your picture.

When we consciously recall the memory of this event, it is like taking out the picture in our minds. Suddenly, the nerves that "aligned" in such a specific way that day scramble into the same formation, and that is when a peculiar thing happens: you actually *feel* it happen again.

Most of us have heard that emotion is strongly connected to our sense of smell, and that is absolutely true. This phenomenon is also observed when we recall memories.

Your mind probably is not that blown by the conclusion of this winding explanation, right? Remember something positive from your past, and you will feel happier for a few moments. Remember something negative, and you will feel sadder. Got it?

If this correlation between memory and emotion were completely unchangeable, then Police Officers would have one more obstacle to deal with when trying to overcome traumatic events from the past.

The reason it matters so much to us, however, is that it thankfully can be tampered with. We can rewire this connection to help reconcile with ourselves after being involved in traumatic events.

Have you ever overcome a taste aversion? Let us say you had an awful first experience with sushi. You got food poisoning, and you spent most of the night, well, you know.

It is not unreasonable to think that after your dismal debut with the raw fish delicacy, you will do just about anything to avoid sushi. Furthermore, even hearing the word "sushi," seeing it plated up half a room away, or especially smelling it, will make you feel sick.

But your friend, the sushi connoisseur who first convinced you to try it, really wants you to appreciate sushi for all of its deliciousness. After apologizing fervently, they beg for one more chance to show you how good sushi really is.

After plenty of protesting, you finally agree to slowly transition from vegetarian sushi (just rice/seaweed) to fully cooked sushi. Then, after four or five good experiences, you finally venture into the authentic stuff.

Lo and behold, it was delicious. You loved every roll you tried, and from that point on, you were a fan.

Now, I do not mean to belittle any traumatic experiences that you have been through. I fully acknowledge that some of the things you may have seen or been a part of are far worse than a bout of food poisoning.

Still, the concept holds. For example, if the last time you discharged your firearm, you harmed or killed someone in the line of duty, that holster is going to feel very heavy on your hip if you do not do something about it. You do not need the added anxiety or stress.

You want to press on and keep doing what you are passionate about. You want to overcome this trauma, but every time you strap on your weapon, you relive that terrible call in your mind.

Here is what you do. Little by little, you must repair the relationship between you and your weapon by using it in controlled, low-stress scenarios. Have some friends and/or colleagues go to the range with you. After you are done "plinking," go out to get some grub with them. Have fun.

Do this enough times, and you will effectively weaken the association between your firearm and the traumatic memory. Just like our friend, who finally came around to sushi.

So, to recap, your brain flash-freezes a particular arrangement of neurons that correspond to everything they sensed during the traumatic (or any other) event. Since your firearm played a vital role in the event, every time you see it, you recreate this awful experience in your head.

In order to overcome this trauma that has formed an association with your firearm, you must create a *new* arrangement of neurons. In essence, you have to associate a more pleasant memory with the firearm to replace the old one.

The stronger the trauma, of course, the more conditioning it will take to overcome it. But do you see just how powerful this can be for law enforcement professionals struggling with depression and PTSD?

If you can identify the negative associations you have made with everyday objects/people/smells or whatever else, you have step one in the bag. Even if it is not related to trauma, every negative thought is a point against your mental wellbeing.

Step two is a bit more nuanced. Reflect on why you do not like these things. Was it something that happened, or just an impression you formed after hearing others talk?

After you have identified what triggers the negative thought and what created it in the first place, you can begin repairing your perception by forming healthier associations with these things.

It is wise to target the big stuff first, like our example of the problem with the firearm, but do not make the mistake of discounting the impact of the little stuff. It all adds up, as they say.

The Operative Word = Active

Have you noticed any consistent themes in the way that the brain operates? Do any of these fickle tendencies point to a clear motive or two?

Efficiency through repetition. Survival. Passing on the genes. Those are the big three.

Your brain wants to automate things. Learn a habit, get really good at it, and practice it often enough to keep that neural connection nice and speedy. Do not go outside; there are "bears" out there. Get fat. Find a compatible partner. Have some kids.

What is more, your brain absolutely loves repetition. For any of you that have kids, you may be nodding your head (and rubbing your forehead as the headache approaches) because boy do those kids show love to leverage repetition.

It is useful, though, because the brain loves it. Doing the same thing repeatedly, especially when there is a tangible reward of food, money, dopamine, protecting the spawn, or what have you, is what your brain wants.

Repetition saves energy. It minimizes the risk of unexpected stressors. It allows your brain to pull out its most shiny and impressive skills to use over and over and over again. See the problem here? As police officers, every single call is a new adventure.

We may romanticize "new adventures" as a species that loves to push the envelope, like going on exotic cruises, bungee jumping, and safaris, but what do most of us feel by the third or fourth day of that excursion?

I want to go home.

Can you imagine your poor brain as a police officer? Even without technology, the simple fact that you might be going to call after call, day in and day out, is stressful enough.

If we just stuck to our brain's default settings as police officers, as many of us who do not care to address our mental health do, then absolutely – we are exposing ourselves to an exponentially higher risk of depression, PTSD, and even suicide.

Why? Think about policing. It is the *exact opposite* of what your brain wants. You are constantly putting yourself in danger. Your mind must work hard to process information carefully when you are approaching potentially hostile people. It cannot relax as often as it wants to.

Our evolutionary blueprint tells us to go right, and we go left – pretty much every time. The result is the impetus for this book: depression, PTSD, addiction, and suicide. It sounds like a grim picture, but thanks to the science of neuroplasticity, it is an opportunity to exercise.

Here is what I mean by "exercise": Just imagine you have put on a solid 5 or 50 unwanted pounds. Are we confused as to how or why that happens in the 21st century? Is it like, "Wow, I must not have worshipped the right gods." These are modern times. We know it is because of beer and chips.

Nevertheless, still, when this happens to the mind, we are stunned and confused. It is much harder to acknowledge and address the more discrete symptoms of mental illness than a belly that literally sticks out for everyone to see.

The point is this: addressing your mental health as a police officer is an *active process.* What is more, it is an ongoing process. You do not just "lose the weight," as it were, and never worry about it again. So long as you are working in the field, you will always, always have to "work out."

You cannot even begin to address your mental health issues, however, if you cannot identify them. That is why the first step is reflection. As I mentioned, you should first identify the real reasons for your negative thought patterns. It may sound simple, but it is not always.

Once you have identified the problem perceptions, you can condition your brain to associate the memories that caused those perceptions with more positive stimulus.

And then you do it again. And again. And again.

This is not a singular problem that you fix. It is a permanent lifestyle change that requires ongoing, active involvement.

I want to conclude this chapter by emphasizing just how powerful of an improvement in your mental wellbeing you can create by using neuroplasticity as your engine of change.

This Is Your Brain on Positive Thinking

As per usual, I will start with the "doom and gloom" first, but then we will round it out with the good news, so stick with me if you would.

Many police officers who do not address their mental wellbeing healthily and appropriately, may feel as though their body is trapped in a survival mentality. They may become selfish and insecure.

It seems like a bit of a vague connection, right? Why do we feel scared, stressed out, and irritable all the time? Well, yeah, those three are, of course, a significant presence, but hear me out for a second.

Back to the beloved Neanderthal analogy. Let us say you stumble out of your cave one morning to find a dire wolf camped out, waiting for you. SNAP – before you know it, the damned thing has clamped down on your ankle, sending a red-alert in the form of searing pain to your brain.

"We aren't going down today," your brain says. "It is survival mode time." Your sympathetic nervous system kicks in. You know the rest – hormones, blood rushing to your muscles, everything moves in slow motion, etc.

Let us say this encounter evolves into a long-winded chase. Every time the wolf gets close, you whip around and fight it off with a club or something.

During this whole episode, and for several hours after (*and remember, the hormones are still in your system*), are you in a balanced and healthy mindset? More specifically, are you thinking about others?

Of course not. You are not thinking about other people or ideas. Your brain is not entertaining abstract thoughts about music or movies or whatever else you like. You do not remember the vacations you have taken.

You may be utterly selfish at that moment because your survival depends on it.

As police officers, this creates problematic thought patterns. Think about it this way: eventually, the scary stimulus goes away. The threat of it, however, is always looming in your mind. And remember, your emotional center cannot tell the difference between the memory of an event and the actual facts of what occurred.

So, what do you do when you have these hormones continuously pumping, but there is no actual threat occurring at that moment?

Well, you become self-obsessed in other, less immediate ways. You have negative thoughts about how people talk to you. You become upset with yourself over your weight, or that mistake you made yesterday, or whatever else.

This is because the hormones of stress place a massive emphasis on our immediate, material surroundings. They whisper to your subconscious, *stop worrying about your long-term goals, and all these other unnecessary thoughts. Just get what you need right now or die.*

It is not that you become a jerk in your conscious mind. You still *want* to be a good spouse or significant other. You want to be a good parent. However, this selfish insecurity driven by your prolonged survival mentality is yet another hurdle in the way.

I have already explained the value of replacing negative associations with positive ones in terms of overcoming negative thought patterns. It is naïve to think, however, that any police officer could completely fortify their mind against the survival mentality.

It is inevitable. It is highly manageable but still unavoidable. Even if you can eliminate nearly all your negative and selfish thought patterns, you cannot rewire your brain's survival drive.

You can, however, insert a new player into the field that will potentially deter the side effects I have just been mentioning – self-obsession and insecurity.

That player is gratitude.

Be thankful for what and who you have. Wake up and meditate on it. Take a moment when you have one to tell your loved ones that you love them. It is not a lie, either. We are so coddled in this era that it is ridiculous. I mean, we hunt *for sport*. When you think about that, it is kind of crazy.

What does gratitude do? It directly contradicts these pesky manifestations of stress hormones. It tells your brain, "No, you do not need to worry about that right now. Worry about it when we're arguing with the next criminal."

And boy, do the possibilities open up when you have mastered gratitude. You can work on yourself more healthily, with a greater emphasis on self-discovery, reflection, ambitions for the future, and creative thinking. You can enter a productive and healthy mentality, even when that threat of danger looms in the background.

I know it sounds a little corny at first, but entering a grateful mentality is the answer to *so* many mental health issues – including but not just depression, PTSD, and anxiety.

I hope after reading this chapter that you have a more intimate understanding of just how malleable and coachable your brain actually is. In some cases, it is a matter of rewiring of negative associations. In others, you are using positive thought patterns to mediate the effects of those stress hormones.

I mentioned briefly that the body and mind maintain a highly important synergy that can make or break your career in law enforcement. Neglect your physical wellbeing, and the brain will suffer. Neglect your mental health, and the body will suffer.

Rather than merely stating the problem, I want to delve much deeper into it because it is so integral to the issue of mental health and suicide risk in the law enforcement community. That said, let us carry on to our chapter about the mind-body connection.

CTA 2:

Write down three healthy techniques, practices, and/or events that you believe help you to reduce stress. Then act upon them and stick with them.

Chapter III: Physical and Mental Stress Go Hand in Hand

"Stress is the general term describing the psychological and bodily response to a stimulus that alters your equilibrium" (Lazarus & Folkman). The emphasis here is on psychological and bodily responses. The second emphasis is on equilibrium.

When we are in what some neurologists would call our "rest state," the brain is happy. All systems are humming along at optimal performance levels. Digestion and metabolism, check. Heart and lungs, check. This is where the brain and body want to be.

Rest state means maintaining a healthy equilibrium in terms of our endocrine (makes all the hormones) and other systems' activity levels. It means that we are not "over-revving" anything, which equals calorie conservation and longevity.

Enter the stressor. When a stressful stimulus threatens your immediate (or long-term, as we will discuss) safety, your brain goes into emergency mode. Hopefully, you have heard the phrase "fight or flight" about the function of the hypothalamus and sympathetic nervous system.

In order to explain these fancy terms, we have to return to our caveman scenario. You walk out into the morning daylight, that wolf snaps its hungry jaws onto your ankle, and boom – your brain is suddenly awash in adrenaline and other natural uppers. Blood is quickly shunted away from your digestive system and to your muscles. Objects in your periphery that you usually ignore suddenly become highly relevant. It is time to run away.

So, let us take a snapshot of the brain at this moment. Five seconds before, you were in a rest state, relaxing and enjoying the woods. Your brain was humming along, making those dozens of micro-calculations that we do not even think about. The sun is here, so it is this early. The wind is blowing from that way. Then, when the wolf chomped your ankle, you were jolted into that hypothalamic reaction violently, throwing your hormones way out of whack. This is a pretty clear-cut example of an acute stressor.

Acute Stressors

As a police officer, of course, we are dealing less with wolves than we are with unstable or otherwise distressed human beings. The concept remains the same, however. When you command someone to put their hands up, and they reach for their waist, you know darn well that a shot of adrenaline is going to hit your bloodstream.

Now, the following distinction is critical. To an extent, acute stressors are healthy. The term *"eustress,"* with *"eu"* meaning "good" if you know your etymology, represents this healthy level of acute stress.

When the stressful stimulus is controlled, for example, as one would experience in a tough workout, a day of mountain biking with friends, a rock concert, and so forth, then the body and mind can handle it reasonably well and move on with little to no residual damage. Eustress.

When the stressful stimulus is severe and unpredictable, however, then acute stress can reap several harmful effects on both the mind and body. "Severe and unpredictable," of course, is not a farfetched prospect as it concerns the daily affairs of police officers on the street. Gang members and drug addicts especially tend to excel in this arena.

So, whether it is a caveman versus a wolf or an officer versus a combative individual, each acute episode will elicit that pre-programmed response of ours. In turn, everything will go into hyperdrive. When these events occur rather infrequently, as mentioned, human physiology is well-equipped to handle the negative stressors.

For example, most civilians will have just a couple of scares a month. Maybe some goofball drifts into your lane on the road, or your 2-year-old decides to take a swan dive off the coffee table. They will have a quick shot of adrenaline, the stressor will be resolved, and ten minutes later they are no worse for the experience.

From an evolutionary perspective, acute stress is easier for us to handle than chronic stress. Think about it: cavemen did not have to worry about their 401k plans and mortgages. They were more concerned with immediate dangers, so Darwin helped them out for a few thousand years.

As mentioned, when a stressful stimulus reaches a certain threshold of severity and unpredictability, it is no longer a healthy stressor. In fact, when a stressor is really a traumatic event, then it can manifest itself acutely and chronically. The brain will recall the trauma and not know the difference between this memory and the actual event, creating chronic stress. Sound familiar? If not, review the previous chapter!

We are going to talk about chronic stress in just a moment. However, for now, I want to illuminate just how damaging acute stressors can be when they exceed the healthy threshold of severity and frequency.

The next chapter will breakdown signs and symptoms of specific states of an unhealthy mind (aka as mental disorders) contributing to suicide risk, like PTSD, anxiety, depression, and so forth. Still, I want to shine the spotlight on PTSD for just a moment because it best illuminates the side effects of unhealthy acute stressors.

Most PTSD sufferers, seeing as it so prominently affects military service members and police, can refer to more than one traumatic event during their service. However, it is very possible and still fairly common to see PTSD develop from a singular event.

That said, an unhealthy acute stressor can bring about all the symptoms that we with PTSD know and hate:

- Sleeping difficulties

- Night terrors

- Flashbacks

- Anxiety attacks

- Avoidance behaviors (avoiding triggers)

- Relationship problems

- Self-harming behaviors

- Trouble concentrating

- Anger and irritability

Unfortunately, this is just a snapshot of the many symptoms of PTSD. More, unfortunately, you can add the symptoms of chronic stress, which I am covering next, to these because of the tendency of people living with PTSD to frequently recall and relive the event.

To not be an absolute downer in every sense of the word, I do need to remind you that this book is going to bring you a solid set of results-based approaches at the end. There is hope at the end of this grimness, but we cannot discuss solutions when we do not know the problems well enough.

Now for the real killer – chronic stress.

Chronic Stress

I will not be so selfish to say that police hold the patent on chronic stress. In fact, there is probably not a single person who has ever made it from birth to death without a few furrows in their brow.

It does not take a rocket surgeon to uncover why chronic stress is such a presence in this type-A culture of ours, especially. We need more money, more stuff, better technology, tastier and less healthy food, and so on. The college grad buying a home is starting life with a quarter-million dollars or more in debt.

While the law enforcement profession did not create chronic stress, it certainly perfected it. Imagine having to deal with all these above issues and always worry about whether or not you are going to be hurt or killed – especially if you have a spouse and/or children.

Okay, you might be thinking, chronic stress is highly prevalent, but why is it worse than acute stress? I mean, is sitting there and worrying worse than being attacked by a dire wolf?

Yes. Literally yes.

Allow me to clarify. No, the "shot" of adrenaline and other fight-or-flight hormones is, of course, not as intense when you are sitting in traffic and wondering if you are the next target of an ambush. But you worry about this and fifteen other things as a police officer all day, every day.

This means that your stress hormones are always on, which is not a great place to be for many reasons. The physiology of our primary systems (i.e., cardiovascular, digestive, endocrine, and so on) begin to breakdown. Why? Because these stress hormones were not meant for long-term use.

As promised, I am not going to dive into the nitpicky details of the physiology. However, I do need to give you at least a general overview of chronic stress physiology so that you can really understand why this is such a pressing issue.

First and foremost is cortisol. Cortisol is a stress hormone that causes a great deal of the problems associated with long-term stress. When that cortisol is swirling around for too long, it throws off our electrolytes, especially sodium. When sodium is off, your heart and other muscles can suffer.

If you are at risk for heart disease, stress is your worst enemy, and this prolonged cortisol action is why. Hereditary risk + chronic stress is virtually a guarantee that you will develop what the previous generations warned you about.

Even if you are not at risk for heart disease, your body uses cholesterol (among other stuff) to make cortisol, and not all of the cholesterol is used up. If you are consistently producing cortisol, then…your turn to do the math.

Additionally, cortisol wants you to have quick access to energy. This makes sense, right? It is a stress hormone, so it is trying to make sure that you can get that "fuel injection" when you need to act quickly in the face of danger on the job. How does it do this? By redistributing what you take in as belly fat, of course.

Another way to ensure that the body has improved access to glucose and other natural fuels is to temporarily remove the player that regulates blood sugar levels: insulin. Again, it makes sense, but it is not so helpful in the chronic context.

Insulin controls blood sugar, but on a stressful call, the body wants fast access to a lot of sugar so that it can chase down and stop the criminal. So, what does pesky cortisol do? Well, it just hits the "off switch" on insulin production. In the acute scenario, 30 seconds or a minute of insulin cessation is pretty much negligible. Cortisol is not the bad guy on its own. We make it the bad guy by never turning it off.

Alas, in the chronic scenario, cortisol ushers our tissues into a state of insulin resistance, which means diabetes.

This is all from one hormone. Moreover, we wonder why we are so unhealthy in this modern age? Stress.

All right, that is enough of the gloomy prognostications. It is time to take an honest look at building a solution. We, of course, cannot alter the nature of the job in an external sense. We cannot eliminate the stressors at the source.

Since we have just learned that a chronically stressed mind can profoundly affect the body, we should at least be wary of the physical stressors we experience on an average day.

See where this is going? The mind-body connection can be leveraged for stress relief from both ends. When you cannot control the craziness of the outside world, you fortify yourself against it by maintaining your physical wellbeing and practicing the strategies discussed in Chapter V. That is why physical wellbeing is just as important in the instance of stress relief. In essence, a strong body contributes to a healthy mind and vice versa.

So, that being said, let us take a look at the physical stressors of the job.

The Dead Weight – Even conservatively, that belt, vest, gun, and all your other gear is going to pack on a solid twenty pounds at least. Whether or not a weighted vest is beneficial for a workout is up for debate, sure, but wearing one all day is unanimously frowned upon by medical professionals. This places undue stress and your neck, back, hips, knees, and ankles.

Don't get me wrong though, you better be wearing that vest!

Rotating and/or Night Shifts - This is a perfect example of a non-traumatic stressor that can still wreak havoc on the mind's hormonal balance. This then contributes to depression and other mental health challenges. Most officers, especially when newer to the force, can identify with this scenario. You are stuck working nights or rotating shifts for who knows how long, and there is not a whole lot you can do about it. Your brain sees that it is dark on your way to work, so it starts pumping those wonderful sleep hormones. Then, as you blast yourself with light and another stimulus throughout the shift, the brain says, "Uh, stop production, I guess?" When it finally *is* time to go to bed, it is light out!

See the problem here? Still, the body and mind are resilient. In essence, the circadian rhythm is capable of shifting, even though it is not an optimal choice. Where you really get into trouble is with the rotating shift. This is when your brain and body enter a state beyond tired and into sheer disarray. The hormones do not know what to do. You feel irritable, depressed, exhausted, and helpless. Some rotating shift workers even report hallucinations. Does that sound like a balanced brain? I remember one night I spotted someone approximately fifty yards away, and then realized as I got close to it, it was a fire hydrant. Do not tell me you have not seen things before!

Sitting – It is kind of an ironic thing to say – that sitting is the new smoking – but the research is really starting to reinforce this idea in a frightening way. Again, police do not hold the patent on prolonged sitting, but they are certainly a part of this group. Sitting for too long can lead to a broad range of minor, moderate, and even life-threatening problems, including:

- Diverticulitis (blood clot)

- Muscle atrophy, strain, and chronic pain

- Increased risk of:

  o Heart attack

  o Stroke

  o Diabetes

  o Cancer

  o <u>Anxiety and Depression</u>

- Weight gain

- Digestive issues

- Osteoporosis

As you can see above, I wanted to really emphasize anxiety and depression, which have been *directly* linked to sedentary lifestyles. The nature of this connection is not yet agreed upon, but what we do know for sure is that there is an association. The leading school of thought here, which I agree with heavily, is that depriving your body of activity is also depriving it of all those "feel good" hormones, called enkephalins and endorphins. It is one less weapon you have to combat those negative thought patterns that contribute to suicide risk.

Eating at Restaurants – Look, we can lay the whole "dougnut" thing to rest. Everybody likes doughnuts. Police officers are not exactly known for making the most health-conscious decisions when eating out at restaurants. Logistically, it is often a necessity to eat at restaurants. So, I am not trying to be all judgmental here – guilty as charged. It all comes down to choices, though. Almost every restaurant has at least a semi-decent option on their menu.

This may sound like the textbook finger-wagging you got from your teachers and your mother for all those years. However, according to a Harvard study, the relationship between food and your mood is much more intimate and delicate than we thought.

Everyone knows that burgers will make you fat. Got it. Nevertheless, did you know that 95 percent of your serotonin production comes from the digestive system and that the food you eat can throw that out of whack? If you take in probiotics (*good bacteria*) that help your stomach's bacterial landscape (*microbiome*) function properly, then you are supporting this serotonin production and optimizing your serotonin levels. If you are eating refined sugars, preservatives, and other crap, you are not only throwing your hormonal balance off – you are inviting a bunch of other problems as well, such as:

- Cancer

- Heart disease

- Alzheimer's and dementia

- Obesity

- Stroke

- Pretty much anything bad that can happen to the body

Seriously. Diet is absolutely central to your mental health. If you absolutely must have a greasy morsel slathered in sauce, at least go for grilled chicken instead of a deep-fried monstrosity or a bacon-topped hamburger.

This is yet another point in yet another chapter where I have to say, "Okay, I promise I am done with the grimness for a moment." Again, I really do not intend to send you running away from your career in law enforcement, screaming.

The takeaway here is not to memorize every single disorder and problem listed above, and then to memorize every single micro-adjustment you can make to prevent them, because that would be darn near impossible. Ironically, it would probably *increase* your stress levels, and I do not need to repeat a fifteenth time just precisely how detrimental stress can be.

"Well, okay, but how do I prevent all this terrible stuff from happening then?" It is indeed a reasonable question. In order to answer it, I want to use an analogy that will hopefully hit close to home.

Mindfulness vs. Panic

It is your first day on the force. You are as green as a blade of grass. Like most rookies, you may want nothing more than to impress your training officer, the other officers in your department, and especially the higher-ups. This is what drives your anxiety in those first few months.

So, you enter a state of hypervigilance. You try your best to soak in every single piece of information that your fellow officers give you. You stop every car that you see. You take mental notes on everything you possibly can.

Knowing what you now know about the physiology of the "rest state" versus a stressed/anxious state, what do you think is happening to your brain in these first few months on the force? Let me rephrase the question: How did you feel after getting home for those first few months?

Tired. Stressed out. Psyched about what you are doing, sure, but definitely tired.

Imagine if you were to maintain this kind of disposition for your entire life! We revere high-level executives, athletes, and other type-A personalities in this country especially, but what we do not often see is the havoc that such a "high RPM" drive wreaks havoc on mental health.

Now, there is a considerable difference between settling in and becoming that jaded officer who makes questionable decisions, but that is a topic for another book entirely.

The point is this: once you are on the force for long enough, your brain combines all those nitpicky data points you were so worried about into a database of user-friendly information. Then, you have a *sense* of what to do instead of constantly worrying about which page of your notes you have to flip to so you can fill out that DWI paperwork.

Sound like a load of bull poop? Here is another way to look at it. Let us say that you (a rookie) and your much more seasoned partner encounter a situation that neither of you have seen before. Your partner is still going to have a better handle on what to do, even though they have never studied for that exact scenario.

Bringing this back around to the topic of the mind-body connection, I am using this metaphor of the rookie officer to make sure that you do not flood yourself with stress and anxiety after reading this book. You ought to find the most effective ways to utilize this information.

Instead of increasing your anxiety because of all these things, I want you to become — here is the kitchy buzz word of the day — mindful of them in a way that is conducive to your physical and mental health.

Think about your "health nut" friends. In my mind, there are two kinds these days. First, the kind that quietly and successfully manage their health using millennia-old methods: sleep, diet, and exercise. These people are doing it right.

Then you have the obsessives. Nothing is good enough. They track every pound daily, and they freak out when they do not meet their goals.

That is the difference between mindfulness and anxiety. What exactly does that look like? Well, how did you lose your rookie anxiety? You just, like, went to work every day. You got over it.

It is okay to be a little stressed out and concerned. Our profession can do some severe damage if you do not care to help yourself — I am not going to lie. Nevertheless, instead of staying in that rookie mentality and just compounding the issues, you are so worried about, put your mind at ease by *practicing* healthier habits.

So far, that means identifying sources of negative thought patterns. It means replacing these negative correlations with positive ones. It means eating healthier food, sitting less (when you can, of course), and optimizing your sleep schedule to the best of your ability.

Once you harness the power of myelination by forming a habit, then you will no longer need to burden yourself with the anxiety that comes with consciously recalling the stressful stuff. Instead of" *I am gonna die if I do not do this," "I am gonna die if I do not do this,"* your brain will just be like, *"Oh hey, it is Tuesday"* as you are going about your day and making better decisions.

A Frank Suggestion, If I May

This next part is a little bit delicate, but necessary. I want to prime you for chapters V and VI, where the real treatments and strategies come into play, by clearing up some of the stigmas surrounding mind-body healing methodology.

So, first and foremost, I want you to know that I do not presume to know your past experiences, your preferences, or your unique health situation. I am not stereotyping you as some overweight, stressed out, jaded officer. Some of us are very fit. Some of us are conservative, others liberal, others unsubscribed.

That being said, it is not exactly a secret that police officers do not much go for complementary and alternative medicine (CAM) treatments. Examples: yoga, meditation, massage, tai chi, etc.

In fact, the social climate in many departments is such that the mere mention of many of these practices might just get you laughed out of the room.

Still, according to the *International Journal of Complementary & Alternative Medicine,* Hatha and forms of yoga and meditation techniques have been objectively proven to dramatically decrease physical and mental stress-related maladies in people with high-stress occupations.

Uh, perfect solution much?

Well, let us not go so far as to say that you will be "one with everything" after three sessions of sweating through every inch of fabric on your body. However, it is fair to say that mind-body medicine is absolutely a large part of the overall solution. Alternatively, it can be, if you but drop your concerns over the stigma and simply try it for yourself.

In a nutshell, I am saying that in order to promote change, you need to frequently seek out resources that you would not have sought out before. Be open-minded.

On the individual level, using healthy, non-pharmaceutical therapies, exercise, meditation, etc. will potentially deter your stress-related issues. On an industry-wide level, if you and your fellow officers band together and make a case to management that you need access to these resources through your job, then something amazing just might happen.

For example, where I used to work, there is a nice weight room and a quality cardio room. Excellent resources for the Officers.

The same article I just referenced above goes on to talk about the organizational change required for criminal justice agencies to smoothly and effectively incorporate wellness programs that address stress-related problems among officers. Even if it is not your job to make those organizational adjustments on your own, you can be on-the-ground to lobby as a conscientious member to kickstart the process.

Bringing It All Together

Alas, this book is not focused on organizational policy changes (thank goodness). We are here to talk about the unacceptable level – as in, more than zero – of police officer suicides. I would like to summarize the key takeaways from this chapter in that context so we can have a clearer picture as we move forward into signs and symptoms.

Here is what we have recently covered:

- Stress is defined as any stimulus, prolonged or acute, that alters your equilibrium in one way or another (cortisol levels and other stress hormones are notable examples).

- You cannot stress the body without stressing the mind, and vice versa. Every stressor elicits a physiological response that involves both the mind and the body to some extent.

- Per above, neglecting either your mental health or your physical wellbeing in even the most seemingly innocent ways can contribute to the cycle of stress.

- Acute stress is manageable to an extent (below severe trauma), but chronic stress is never good. Both forms of stress can contribute to PTSD-like symptoms, including:

  o Sleep difficulties/nightmares

  o Difficulty focusing

  o Impaired communication and relationship management abilities

  o Anger and irritability

  o Flashbacks and anxiety episodes

  o Impaired digestion

  o Obesity

  o Severely increased risk of heart disease, stroke, and brain disorders.

- We cannot eliminate all contributors to chronic stress, like the threat of harm, but we can mediate many of the day-to-day stressors, like prolonged sitting, poor diet, etc.

- Finally, it is crucial to maintain a balanced, mindful perspective of your mental wellbeing to avoid the pitfall of making your health worse by stressing about it constantly. This requires making positive changes (i.e., yoga, improved diet, meditation) into *habits*.

All that tarrying on in this chapter when I simply could have said, "A strong body equals a strong mind." In all seriousness, that is, of course, true, but it does not give us actionable, day-one steps.

Will today be your day one?

If you need help knowing where to start in terms of self-assessment, I have compiled a comprehensive list of common signs and symptoms of the major disorders I keep mentioning (depression, addiction, PTSD, anxiety, etc.) below. Arm yourself with this information, and you will be ready for any treatment.

CTA 3:

Have a family member or friend keep you informed, if need be, of major need-to-know incidents, but do not watch the news for thirty days. See if you feel better mentally because of it. You're welcome.

Chapter IV: Signs and Symptoms of Suicide Risk

Male or female officer, rookie or veteran, it does not matter – we are all affected by the social norms that govern our profession. Police officers are supposed to be stoic and even unfeeling in highly tense situations. We are supposed to be super tough, and we do not need to be thanked or appreciated.

Says the status quo, anyway.

Do not get me wrong; these social norms do have some "adaptive value." What I mean by that is, "cadets" are conditioned long before they join the force to believe that they need to take on this hard exterior. It actually helps their day-to-day functioning when they eventually get started.

This warrior-like "Billy Bada**" socialization, however, has a pretty hefty downside. In fact, the focus of this book is set squarely in this area. Being brought up like this in your career field tends to remove your incentive to acknowledge your problems.

If you get clocked in the face by some "wannabe" tough criminal that you eventually "gained control of", different story. That is more of a badge of honor.

But depression? Fear? Helplessness? Warriors do not talk about that. Warriors are not supposed to be affected by that. See where I am going with this?

Discussing the specific signs and symptoms that indicate suicide risk among police would be a fruitless venture if we did not first demolish that wall that is in our way: the socially driven incentive to ignore your mental health issues.

I do not mean to get all "tough love" on you, but sometimes it takes a bit of a jolt to break through these barriers, so here we go:

You are not "tough." You will never be tough, because the concept does not exist. The only difference between General

Patton and the wimpiest person you know is the ability to conceal the fact that they are terrified.

So, drop the tough guy or tough girl shtick, because short of a psychotically deranged mind, it is not an attainable quality for humans. Fear is programmed into us as an evolutionary protector, and trying to rewire yourself on *that* level is like trying to walk through a wall.

Point? Accept that you are scared, (possibly) depressed, or otherwise affected by your experiences. Acknowledge that everything is not okay. Admit that you have been affected by the things you have seen.

You are not beneficial to your department if you fail to accept these things and end up unable to do your job or worse. Besides, getting the help you need will drastically improve your health, your relationships, and your general outlook on life.

I want you to really meditate on this first part. I know it sounds like the type of "soft skill" mumbo-jumbo that you would find on some natural healing site, but that does not mean it is not absolutely essential for you to overcome these issues.

Now, even if you insist that you are in fact ok, then keep reading because remember, this process of staying ok is continuous!

Ok back on track, so you have accepted the fact that you are not okay. Step one, check. The next logical step, of course, is to assess your specific signs and symptoms so that you can best identify and address the problem on your own.

I know this might sound a tad arrogant, seeing as you are not a mental health professional, but remember what I said earlier: You are the one who provides the theory before the diagnosis. You are the one who sees something wrong, researches the issue, and decides to make the call for help.

Sound sensible enough? Alright – that is quite enough preamble. We are now going to take a good look at the signs and symptoms of suicide risk, which is mostly comprised of depression, PTSD, anxiety disorders, addiction, and substance abuse, and, more directly, suicidal thoughts.

What to Look for When Self-Assessing

It only fits that we kick off this list of signs and symptoms with depression, one of the leading causes of suicide.

Depression

Like autism or even something more physical like multiple sclerosis, depression exists on a spectrum. To a degree, everyone feels depressed at one time or another. For many of us, it is episodic – like during the wintertime (i.e., seasonal affective disorder) or after a particularly tragic event.

Simply feeling depressed for a short while, however, as when grieving, is not technically depression from a mental health perspective. Professional opinions vary, but many specialists require the presence of specific "biochemical markers" as objective evidence that there is a chemical imbalance in the brain.

Aside from looking at key neurotransmitters, receptors, and other mood-regulating elements within the brain, clinicians also acknowledge a small set of other factors. I want you to be aware of factors, such as:

- Family history of depression.

- Day-to-day activities: this is where police score very poorly because they are involved in, or witnessed acts of violence, the aftermath of self-harm, and so on are strong contributors to depression risk.

- Other risk factors include anxiety and low self-esteem.

Most of us are well aware of depression's primary symptom: feeling sad. But how do you know if you are just "regular sad," per above, or actually depressed? In order to equip yourself with the knowledge necessary to make this distinction, you need to appreciate the lesser-known symptoms as well.

Here begins our list of symptoms for depression, excluding the apparent symptom of sadness:

1. Tense, Sore Muscles

This marks the first of many mentions in this chapter about the interplay between depression and anxiety. Know for now that depressed people spend a lot of time worrying whether or not they have been diagnosed with an official anxiety disorder.

What happens on a physiological level when we worry? Well, a lot more than you may think, but for the current purpose, your muscles hold an unhealthy degree of tension. Your facial muscles especially tend to seize up and stay there for too long.

Ever get that pesky eye twitch that does not want to go away? That is just the start. Depression sufferers have reported all-over body aches at times. This can be puzzling for clinicians, especially if they are unaware of the depression because this issue eludes most conventional screening methods.

2. Asocial Tendencies

Indulge me for just one moment while I air out one of my pet peeves:

Asocial people feel indifferent towards others, so they withdraw from society.

Antisocial people feel anger and hostility towards others, so they both withdraw from society and act aggressively towards others.

If you already knew that, great. I just wanted to clear this distinction up because so many people use the wrong term.

So, we are talking about withdrawing from social scenarios and spending more time by yourself. This depression system plays from many other issues related to depression in several ways.

For example, if you also suffer from low self-esteem, which is understandably common, you may feel that you are a burden to others, or that you are not interesting enough to deserve their conversation, etc.

If you feel tragically affected by a history of child abuse, loss of family members, or your experiences in law enforcement, you may feel nobody can relate to you. Trauma victims who experience their trauma alone are especially apt to feel this way.

The dangerous thing about asocial tendencies is that they are self-perpetuating in nature. Withdraw from society for long enough, and you will not know how to re-enter, even if you want to one day. As a result, you will just stay withdrawn and feel more depressed. I do not want you to get to that point, and neither does anyone else!

After enough withdrawal, your ability to perceive yourself objectively will weaken, opening opportunities for you to go down dangerous paths (i.e., radicalization, anti-social behaviors, self-harm, etc.)

3. Impulsivity

A study featured on the US National Library of Medicine National Institutes of Health website sheds some interesting and unfortunate insights on the correlation between severe depression and impulsivity.

First, let us start with a bit of clarification. When it comes to impulsivity, depression often takes a back seat to bipolar disorder. It is easy to set these two conditions at opposite ends of the impulsivity spectrum because that is just how our brains like to do things.

"Well, she is depressed but not bipolar, so I am not so concerned about any manic episodes and/or impulsive decisions in her daily life."

This lack of concern is not merited at all, says the research. The study in reference involved 127 patients who were administered a test that measures impulsivity (called the Impulsivity Rating Scale, or IRS) over a 4-week treatment window.

Long story short, the study found that severely depressed people experience multiple forms of impulsivity that can cause them to make rash decisions. Pair that with severe depression, and you have got a potent boost to suicide risk.

Still, it takes much more than merely feeling really sad and being impulsive to commit to taking your own life. I want you to think of suicide and suicide risk as non-linear things. It is not just, "Well, I am only 40 percent sad, but poor Jon Doe, who killed himself last month, must have been 100 percent sad."

Instead, consider suicide as a very, very bad decision that requires a precise and normally unlikely alignment of *many* factors. Severe depression, feeling withdrawn from society, losing your relationships, and now objectively provable impulsivity are just four among a couple dozen suicide decision factors.

Why am I getting so analytical? Because the more symptoms you recognize, the more substantial chunk you can take out of this problem. If we are to swallow it whole, we need to move on to more signs and symptoms.

4. Fatigue

This is a very, very commonly overlooked sign. I mean Police Officers are tired all the time, right? Stressed out, up and down, filling out paperwork, and so forth.

But what about weekends? What about after a couple days off for holidays? Do you still feel exhausted the whole time? Are you sleeping more than a couple hours during the day?

If you said yes, then you may be experiencing fatigue as a symptom of depression, not just a busy schedule. Unfortunately, this is one of those symptoms that can create more symptoms (e.g., compromised immunity and impaired work performance).

You know what fatigue is, so I am not going to break the concept itself down any further. I just want to emphasize that it is *not okay* to feel tired absolutely all the time. You should feel tired before bed, sure, but do not become complacent with constant fatigue. There is a difference.

5. Anger

While it is not entirely outlandish when you stop to think about it, "anger" still is not the first or second word that pops into mind when most of us think about depression. In fact, our understanding of this connection is so limited, the Diagnostic and Statistical Manual of Mental Disorders (DSM), which is the end-all-be-all resource for psychologists and other mental health professionals, does not even include anger as a symptom of depression.

We strongly suspect they are connected, and we have a couple of theories as to why, but that is about it. Let me walk you through the leading schools of thought.

Remember that "warrior socialization" I talked about earlier? The image of the tough, unfeeling police officer that discourages us from talking about or even acknowledging our mental health problems.

Think of it as a kind of a spectrum that warps the real feeling, sadness, and helplessness, into a more socially acceptable manifestation: anger.

It is more in line with the warrior image, for example, to slam your fist on the dinner table than it is to start crying and talking about your feelings.

This goes double for men. Police Officer or not, men, in general, are expected to possess warrior-like strength and resolve to a certain degree. As such, their subconscious assimilates any feelings of sadness or helplessness, into anger for reasons of social acceptability.

So, there are two critical takeaways with this one. First, know that anger that persists for long periods of time, and to the extent that affects daily function, is *not* just a product of stress or lack of sleep. It could mean you are depressed.

Also, I want to take this moment to emphasize the intricate overlays we see between anger, stress, depression, anxiety, and fatigue. The mind is a tricky organ – you cannot just send a scope up there and take a picture like with bodily issues. Appreciate the fact that your symptoms could be related to more than one disorder.

Now let us move onto tendencies:

1. Difficulty Sleeping

As if you needed another half-explained mystery, we arrive at the issue of sleep.

Look, even if I just copped out on this one – no pun intended - and quoted three or four paragraphs from the experts, you would be even more confused because the opinions vary so widely.

For that reason, I am going to keep it very general so as not to misinform you.

If you sleep too much (hypersomnia), too little (insomnia), or one and then the other, your symptoms may be related to depression. If you feel exhausted during the day to the point of napping frequently, you are in this category as well.

Depression has even been linked by the Sleep Foundation to cause sleep apnea, the condition in which you periodically stop breathing in your sleep.

To further complicate things, the causal relationship between sleep and depression is not clear in every case, either. What I mean by that is, there are unrelated physical conditions that cause insomnia or hypersomnia, and depression can occur as a result of these symptoms.

On the other hand, you can be an otherwise healthy sleeper before your depression. Still, then the depression causes you to experience the aforementioned sleep issues.

The single piece of objective evidence that I *can* confidently introduce into this equation is the issue of serotonin. Remember how I said that clinicians use specific chemical imbalances in the brain as a way of diagnosing depression? Those same imbalances, especially when they involve serotonin (which is highly prevalent), can affect sleep because serotonin regulates sleep, among other functions.

2. Suicidal Thoughts

The big one. The target of this book. Never just welcome these thoughts.

Also referred to as "suicidal ideation," this symptom is very easy to describe. If you think about planning and/or committing suicide, even if it just feels like a passing whim, you are practicing suicidal ideation.

First and foremost, here is the **National Suicide Prevention Lifeline number**:

1-800-273-8255

You absolutely cannot hesitate to call if you ever find yourself considering suicide. I am here to keep you from getting to that point, but that does not mean you do not use this resource if you ever find yourself in that mindset.

Alright, moving on. I said that suicidal ideation is easy to describe, and indeed it is. Yet, it is a bit harder to fully understand in terms of the factors that create this thought process.

For example, reference the above discussion on impulsivity. I mentioned that suicidal actions are more than the simple product of "feeling really sad." It requires a cocktail of many ingredients, one of which is impulsivity.

What else contributes to suicidal ideation? A fascination with violent movies, sports, and real-life events. Drug and alcohol use. Strong feelings of guilt, loss, or regret. Extreme anger or anxiety. Mood swings, whether they are part of a disorder or a natural personality trait. Social isolation. Negative self-talk and/or low self-esteem.

(Ok, take a deep breath and smile, because I know I just listed a lot of negative factors.)

This is not the entire list, but it represents most of the "usual suspects" as it concerns causes for suicidal thought patterns. I want to lay the critical takeaways on you so that you can 1) recognize suicidal thought patterns if and/or when they arise, and 2) know that you have multiple options for preventing and treating them.

Takeaway #1: Only a small percentage of people with suicidal thoughts attempt suicide, and only a small percentage of them succeed.

Takeaway #2: Depression is debatably the most treatable mental illness in existence, even in severe cases.

Takeaway #3: It takes more than sadness and helplessness to form suicidal thoughts, per above. If you routinely feel this way, you will not develop suicidal thoughts without the other mood-affecting traits (impulsivity, low self-esteem, isolation, etc.)

The final takeaway is to know that there are volumes upon volumes of preventive strategies and treatments to keep you from having (or following through on) suicidal thoughts. That will be the focus of the next two chapters, so, for now, let us continue this list of mental health disorders that contribute to officer suicide, because it is crucial you know this.

PTSD

We talked about manageable acute stressors just a short while ago. As police officers, these can take many forms, such as approaching a stranger's driver's side door, intervening in or responding to domestic abuse calls, drug overdoses, and so on, and even dealing with the stress of policies and paperwork in between.

We have already established that your brain is running on caveman 1.1 software at the very best. Nevertheless, the good news is that acute stressors are covered in this outdated tech because of, you know, wolves and bears and ice ages and stuff.

However, this ability of ours has a limit. There is a threshold severity that the stimulus must stay under if it is to be overcome by the body's natural response to it. What happens when the event exceeds that threshold? It becomes trauma, which is likely to cause PTSD.

As one of the most war-involved nations in history, we are no strangers to Post-Traumatic Stress Disorder. Even those lucky enough to not experience it firsthand have likely known somebody who has experienced PTSD.

In a nutshell, PTSD is a condition characterized by various forms of psychological distress following one or multiple traumatic events. Generally, graphic violence, sudden loss of a loved one, and sexual abuse are the most common causes.

I can tell you based on personal experience (based on combat deployments), it feels like it will sneak up on you. If you do not address it and get treatment for it, it can be a tough road ahead.

"Seeing action" in a military sense is a prevalent cause of PTSD, and I am sure you have known someone returning from duty that displayed symptoms.

The only downside to all the much-needed attention that our returning troops are getting is that the PTSD resources for police departments are often relegated to a blurb or two here and a pamphlet there.

If you are interested in the organizational policy side of mental health in the area of law enforcement, Lexipol has published a solid spread on the matter using the experience and expertise of licensed psychotherapist Karen Lansing.

As a representative of the American Academy of Experts in Traumatic Stress, Lansing has toured dozens of departments across the country while helping law enforcement officers cope with PTSD. While she mentions in the article that there were a few departments in her tour that stood out in terms of PTSD-savvy treatment and education, her overall assessment pointed to a lack of preparedness in most law enforcement agencies.

On an individual level, you have the opportunity – as some would say, the obligation – to both advocate for greater access to PTSD resources and make the necessary adjustments in your own situation to improve your outlook.

You cannot really seize either of these opportunities, however, if you do not know what to look for. In the same spirit as our list of depression symptoms, I will highlight some of the lesser-known PTSD symptoms to minimize the chance that you will let the issue slip by.

1. Flashbacks, Nightmares, and Anxiety Attacks

I am grouping these together because the same PTSD sufferer may experience all three of these at different times, and each of these problems stem from the same root: reliving the trauma.

Let us say that you arrived at the scene of a grisly homicide. I will spare you the details, but let us just say that it is very graphic.

Remember that whole "when you experience an event, your neurons align in a super-specific way, creating a memory" thing? Well, when you open that bedroom door and see the most terrible thing you have ever seen, your brain will absolutely sear that into your memory because of the emotional reaction.

That is why people remember where they were on JFK assassination day, or 9/11 – the potent connection between emotion and memory is a little too effective.

So, this terrible image is flash-cooked into your brain, and now you have to deal with reliving it. Anything distinct about that scene, even seemingly innocent stuff like the person's shoes, something in their bedroom, the smell of their apartment, or whatever else, can now become a potential trigger.

When you see that pair of shoes or whatever else you associated with the trauma, it triggers your brain to recreate that alignment of nerves. Then you have to actually *relive* the trauma again and again.

And that is just the semi-conscious side of the anxiety attacks and flashbacks you have when awake. Unfortunately, you do not always need a trigger, as when having a nightmare that is centered on the trauma.

In short, the trauma itself is not actually the worst part. Your brain, the world's best association machine, cannot help but return to that memory when it is prompted (or even when it is not). It is a primary focus of PTSD treatment to decrease the frequency and intensity of these episodes.

2. Avoidance Behavior

It is only fitting at this junction, now that we have covered the concept of PTSD triggers, to move on to avoidance behavior.

Your brain actually has a limited ability to "blockout" specific memories, but when that adaptation is not enough, the PTSD sufferer will often take a more deliberate, conscious approach.

Well, just do not go to violent movies anymore. Stop playing that video game. Move your gun safe out of your room. These are all measures PTSD sufferers will take to stay away from triggers.

This is a bit of a double-edged sword when it comes to effectiveness. On the one hand, sure – out of sight, out of mind. On the other hand, however, we have two problems:

1) Simply avoiding triggers does not actually repair the damage, even though it can provide temporary damage control.

2) Of all people, you deserve to live your life after what you have been through. You should not have to avoid things that you enjoy, which can be a cause of depression in itself. Heck when I came back from Iraq I did not want to go to the beach! Sand!!

It is also important to note that avoidance behavior is relatively easy to justify, which prevents you from getting the help you really need.

I am just tired. I will catch up with you guys next time.

This is why we need the complete picture. This is why we need to appreciate the synergy at work with all these symptoms. Avoidance behavior alone is not enough for a diagnosis.

3. Lack of Emotional Response

What you enjoyed before PTSD; you may not get excited about it anymore. Whether it is something petty like your favorite burger joint or something much more significant, like your relationship with your spouse and/or kids, this can be seriously problematic.

Family is crucial here. They are the ones who know you well enough to have the revelation, "Huh, after his incident at work, he does not really seem to care about going fishing anymore." They are the ones who can get the ball rolling in terms of diagnosis, treatment, and your own personal strategies.

It may seem strange, but you may not even be aware of this issue, which is why the people you are close to are such an essential piece of the puzzle.

So, why does this happen? As promised, I am not going to dive too deep into the neurochemical babble, so allow me to continue with my generalities.

In the case of PTSD, your brain is actually running in a state of hyperarousal. Since your brain cannot tell the difference between the memory and the experience itself, every time you bring it to mind, your body gets ready for action.

Your muscles tense up, your brain demands a higher blood supply to quickly process any imminent threats, your adrenaline pumps, and so forth. In the case of chronic and/or severe PTSD, this situation can go from on and off a few times a day to a semi-permanent state of being.

We will talk more about hyperarousal next, but I had to mention it now to explain why a PTSD sufferer would seem indifferent to things they used to enjoy. It makes sense, right? Your brain is subconsciously reliving a trauma and preparing your body to fight or fly. When it is in that mode, it files everything (*even the important stuff like family*) that is not a lethal threat into the "non-essential, we will deal with it later" category.

4. Hyperarousal

Since I have already warmed this one up for you, I will make the introduction brief. The term hyperarousal refers to the state your brain enters when it is threatened, as in a violent confrontation.

We want to have this capability, do not get me wrong – lifting cars off of pinned children and whatnot. When you *live* there, however, it is like redlining your car every time you drive it. That engine is going to give out before its time.

With the above considered, you should have an easier time understanding and identifying issues related to hyperarousal, which include:

- Being easily startled by loud noises and flashing lights
- Inability to concentrate
- Irritability or anger
- Impulsive behavior
- Poor work performance and interest in social/family activities
- Stomach pain, headaches, and sleep disturbances

Put most simply, these are the things that would happen to you if that intense thirty-second fight you were involved in with a criminal lasted for days upon days. Unfortunately, as outlandish as that concept seems, this is what PTSD sufferers have to deal with.

5. Memory Issues

This one is a doozy and two-fold at that. The first issue involves a little "short circuit" in your brain's memory of the trauma itself, and the second problem involves general memory loss. Let us start with the trauma part.

Remember, Dr. Lansing from before? The psychotherapist and PTSD expert who worked hands-on with law enforcement officers across the country? She explained why the brain replays such a terrible memory more elegantly than I could:

"The brain is aware that the officer has not learned all that he/she needs to know…which is why it keeps pushing the incident up to the surface in dreams…"

A little context to complete this thought. What Dr. Lansing is describing is the phenomenon unique to PTSD sufferers that involves the inability of the brain to identify and evaluate crucial data that could be used to prevent the event from recurring.

That was a "a lot to unpack." Here is what that means: fool me once, shame on you, fool me twice, shame on me. Why is it "shame on me" the second time? Because the brain recognizes the warning signs from the first time so that it will not be hoodwinked again.

In PTSD, however, the brain does not know how to do that. It just cannot translate the sensory information surrounding the trauma into "oh okay, if you see or hear or smell *xyz* again, just do this, and you will avoid it next time."

But the brain still really wants to protect you, so what does it do? It just plays the traumatic memory on a loop, as kind of a confused, last-ditch effort to impart new information that could maybe help you survive. So, yes, it is a memory problem that causes you to continually remember something you do not want to.

Conversely, plain old memory loss is a highly prevalent symptom among PTSD sufferers. It may be as innocuous as one too many "where did I put my keys?" or it could devolve into more severe and long-term memory loss.

6. Negative and Paranoid Thought Patterns

When we discussed hyperarousal just now, we covered a few of the physiological processes that prepare your body for serious action. Your muscles tense up, yadda yadda.

That is all good and fine in terms of what your body is doing, but since law enforcement officers with PTSD are stuck in this state, what does that do to their thought patterns? You cannot just be thinking, "Oh crap, duck!" for hours on end.

Consider what your brain wants to do in this state. It wants to protect itself, the heart, the lungs, and, preferably, everything else above all costs. Depending on the threat, this might mean hurting or killing another living thing.

Do you think that this kind of mentality is conducive to patient, creative, fun, or otherwise abstract thought patterns? No. Here is what your brain is telling you:

The world is a very dangerous place.

It's them or you.

Don't trust anyone. They are all out to hurt you.

You have to do this on your own. Don't let your guard down.

This is also why PTSD, like depression, encourages asocial behaviors. When you feel like you are drowning in a river, you become far too self-obsessed to worry about hanging out with friends. Not like, "Oh, look at me. I'm so cool," self-obsessed, but more like, "What the heck is wrong with me?" self-obsessed.

It is probably apparent to you already that mental health is very much a fluid concept with a lot of overlap in terms of symptomatology. This is why it is much more difficult to screen for and diagnose depression/PTSD/anxiety than it is to test for an ACL tear.

I am mentioning this now because, as we transition into anxiety disorders, you will notice even more similarities between symptoms of "the big three" affecting law enforcement (depression, PTSD, anxiety).

It is only human nature to try and place each of these disorders into distinct boxes. Let me tell you early on that this is fruitless. This is why mental health professionals are educated and trained to the extent that they are – it takes a lot of training and insight to make the distinctions necessary for accurately targeted treatment.

That said, do not worry if it is hard to tell the difference between these big three at first glance. It is more important that you acknowledge that there is a problem in the first place.

Anxiety

First off, I want to emphasize that not all anxiety disorders are created equal. Some people are not even aware that there is more than one anxiety disorder, sadly. You may have just heard this from those who have a disorder:

"I have anxiety."

Like so many other mental health issues, anxiety is not a monolith. It exists on a spectrum.

The U.S Department of Health and Human Services website has a nice, concise breakdown of the five most commonly addressed points on that spectrum.

1. Generalized Anxiety Disorder

Hence the name, this is non-specific. You feel anxious for no apparent reason. Usually a chronic condition.

2. Obsessive-Compulsive Disorder (OCD)

The belief that performing certain actions repeatedly will help to prevent or resolve the anxiety-causing thoughts and memories that keep surfacing.

3. Panic Disorder

A more severe and episodic form of anxiety involving panic attacks. You may suddenly feel short of breath, dizzy, and sick to your stomach for no reason (or with a trigger).

4. Post-Traumatic Stress Disorder (PTSD)

You already know what this is, but did you know it is included under the umbrella of anxiety disorders? See what I mean by overlap?

5. Social Anxiety Disorder

Feeling anxious in even the most casual of social situations. Frequently, the anxiety is specific to certain actions (public speaking, chatting with a stranger, etc.). Still, in more severe cases, it may encompass all social interactions.

Why harp on the distinction between the different anxiety disorders? Because the more you know about each mental health issue, the more you will be able to distinguish it from its seemingly identical counterparts – and that means finding the strategies/treatments you need versus stringing the problem along.

In that spirit, I want you to consider the following list of symptoms in the context of the anxiety spectrum, not just the oversimplified "I have anxiety, and that's it" context. That being said, let us get to arming ourselves with this critical knowledge.

1. The Obvious

Just like depression, most of us know firsthand what it is like to feel anxious from time to time, disorder, or not. The primary symptom of anxiety disorders is, well, anxiety.

Whether it is absolutely all the time or in episodes, you worry excessively. You fear that something is going to happen to you or your family. You think you will be fired. You are worried about your health. Whatever it is, you do not need an excuse to worry about it.

Let us define "excessive" worrying, though, because it will help us separate those of us without anxiety disorders from those of us with anxiety disorders.

Consider it from a survival value standpoint. When a generally non-anxious person experiences anxiety, it is at least partially merited. Maybe they really are going to get fired. Maybe they really do have a potentially serious health problem.

When there is little or no evidence to reinforce the anxious thoughts, however, we may be looking at an anxiety disorder. That said, an anxious person is not always a delusional person. There may still be a factual basis for their worry. However, if their resulting anxiety persists for too long and/or interferes with their health, it is still an anxiety disorder.

2. New Phobias

To clarify, not all who have phobias have anxiety, and not all who have anxiety have specific phobias. There is a subset of anxiety sufferers, however, who focus their anxiety on particular objects or activities.

For example, someone who was never agoraphobic (avoiding places that may cause anxiety/panic) before may develop this potentially life-altering phobia after they develop their anxiety disorder. Agoraphobia is especially common among anxiety sufferers because it combines both an irrational fear with social avoidance behavior, as we will cover below.

Speaking of, not all agoraphobic people shut themselves in the house all day, every day. Some of them will still go out into the world, but they will avoid dense thickets of people, as with public transportation, the grocery store, and so forth.

I am telling you this for two reasons: 1) So you understand that general anxiety can manifest itself in specific ways, and 2) to demonstrate that the same symptom may present itself differently for each person.

3. Irritability

When you include depression and PTSD, Police Officers are three for three on irritability as a symptom of mental health issues.

As much as I loved the world of patrol police work, I cannot help but think that the underlying cause of the irritability is because of the irritating nature of the job.

Mindlessly filling out paperwork, staying up into the wee hours of the morning, dealing with not-so-wholesome individuals – this is why law enforcement is fueled by a passion for helping people and action. Without that, who would want to do this? I know I would not.

Point being, the job itself can be irritating, so it is highly likely that this symptom will surface, whether in depression, anxiety, or PTSD.

4. Trouble Concentrating

Like PTSD, anxiety interferes with short-term memory, a key component to concentration.

Also, like PTSD, the fact that your brain is essentially stuck in survival mode, or at least halfway between rest state and survival mode, does not bode well for your higher-level cognitive functions.

Remember: When you are in that state, it is all about "run, smash, survive" versus "hm, I wonder how x and y are related." See the difference?

What I mean is, when it comes to concentration and memory, the anxiety sufferer is both directly and indirectly affected by the disorder, making it much tougher.

That being said, if the task in reference is something you have done a million times, you will have an easier time with it.

5. Fatigue

When it comes to the relationship between anxiety and fatigue, I like to use a "slow drip" versus a "shot" metaphor.

As mentioned, Police Officers have to deal with both chronic and acute stressors. You are chronically worried about paperwork, emails, social notifications, the threat of harm, and so forth. Then there is being acutely worried when threats are detected while on calls.

Now to the physiological component. When you have chronic anxiety or generalized anxiety disorder (GAD), your stress hormones are on a slow drip, as though you have taken medications at the hospital.

This means that, while your heart may not be thumping out of your chest. You may not be gasping for air all day, you are still in a state of hyperarousal that keeps your body running above its optimal level. This creates a pretty massive "energy debt" that results in fatigue.

In the "shot" scenario, we are talking about panic attacks. Even if you do not have an anxiety disorder, you can still have a panic attack if something goes wrong on a call, and you fear for your life or the lives of those around you.

So, in this case, your body absolutely floods itself with a wave of stress hormones. I mentioned that this is the "preferred" form of stress, as the body is more accustomed in an evolutionary sense to dealing with acute stressors. The caveat in law enforcement, however, is that these acute stressors are too intense and too frequent.

The result? Among other things, fatigue.

6. Social Withdrawal

This is anxiety's proprietary flavor of avoidance behavior. Like with depression, anxiety sufferers will often avoid social situations, but it is usually to prevent panic attacks or at least the intensification of anxious feelings.

Let me phrase it this way so that you can better distinguish between these two very similar forms of avoidance behavior (depression-related social withdrawal versus anxiety-related social withdrawal).

Here is the social avoidance thought process with depression:

Why would they want to hang out with me? I am not worth it. Besides, I do not have fun anyway. It does not matter.

Here is the social avoidance thought process with anxiety:

What if someone asks me a personal question, and I freak out? What if they can see how crazy I am? What if nobody likes me? What if what if what if?

I do not mean to poke fun at anxiety sufferers. But, exaggeration is sometimes the best way to illuminate a point.

Even if a person does not have social anxiety, they may still experience increased anxiety from simply going out in the world, driving, waiting in line somewhere, trying a new restaurant or movie they are not sure about, and so on and so forth.

I will not speak for psychotherapists and other mental health professionals. Still, in my mind, the three conditions we have discussed so far almost completely encompass the mental health concerns faced by law enforcement professionals.

By now, you should understand that the decision to commit suicide is far more nuanced than we make it out to be. It requires a precise combination of self-esteem issues, helplessness, isolation, impulsivity, and an overall lack of critical coping mechanisms.

Even in the absence of trauma and chronic stress, drug and alcohol abuse can significantly increase your chances of developing depression, anxiety, and, ultimately, suicidal ideation.

The link between substance/alcohol abuse and mental illness runs so deep, in fact, that clinicians and researchers have to contend with the issue of causality here. Was it the drug abuse that caused the depression, or the depression that caused the drug abuse?

Tackling this question, as always, requires an informed approach. Let us take a look at the known causes, correlations, signs, and symptoms of substance addiction and abuse.

Alcoholism

This one is, unfortunately, muddled by cultural norms, especially in the United States. What I mean by that is, many of our dominant subcultures (football fandom, college kids, corporate employees, and oh lordy, nurses and teachers) uphold binge drinking as a longstanding rite.

See the problem here? Binge drinking is woven into our culture, which is the perfect camouflage for the real alcoholics to blend in with.

Sources differ in terms of the criteria required for one to be labeled an alcoholic. Some emphasize quantity, such as the number of drinks in a night/week/month, others underline the lack of ability to function without it, and some blend the two.

I prefer the Mayo Clinic definition, which includes the following behaviors:

- Being preoccupied with the need to drink, both during, before and after drinking sessions

- Persistent abuse of alcohol even after it starts to cause problems

- Requiring more alcohol to achieve the same level of drunkenness

- Experiencing withdrawal symptoms between drinking sessions (irritability, headaches, trouble concentrating, etc.)

More importantly, for our mission, we are going to explore the connection between alcoholism and suicide risk. After all, it is literally in the name. Alcohol is classified as a depressant, so the connection is not a vague one.

That being said, let us take a look at the symptoms of alcohol addiction before we explore this connection further.

1. Unhealthy Fluctuations in Weight

This particular symptom can vary (weight gain versus weight loss) based on individual preference. Still, the premise remains the same across all types of drinkers: alcohol takes precedence over food.

The nature of the weight fluctuation, then, depends on the kind of alcohol and the change in eating habits that alcoholism has brought about.

For example, if the drink of choice for an alcoholic is (non-light) beer, then the sheer quantity that they would have to drink and the higher density of calories means that we are looking at a likelihood of significant weight gain in a short period of time, even with the neglecting of nutritionally dense food sources.

Conversely, someone who prefers hard liquor without any sugary soda to mix it with is actually more likely to lose weight if they also prioritize the alcohol over food. This is because, while they are imbibing far more than the safe amount of alcohol, they will be drinking a lower quantity of less calorically dense drinks than the beer "enthusiast" while limiting their food intake.

2. Dehydrated Skin, Hair and Nails

You do not have to be a card-carrying alcoholic to overdo it at that wedding or work function once or twice a year, but boy will you feel the dehydration the next morning.

Your lips are chapped painfully, your skin feels like sandpaper, and your eyes might even hurt. These are all pretty obvious symptoms of dehydration, which alcohol is a master of.

Here is your word of the day: diuretic. This refers to a class of compounds (alcohol and caffeine among them) that cause your kidneys to release more water than they normally do. This is because diuretics fight the hormones that prevent too much water from releasing the kidney.

Remember: Alcohol = dehydration. I have felt it too, not fun.

3. Craving and Withdrawal

Largely agreed upon as one of the hallmark attributes of alcoholics, I am also of the belief that the craving, consumption and withdrawal cycle is the most crucial indicator of this disease.

Especially for alcoholics in law enforcement, cravings can be intensified when stressful things happen at work. You crave it and crave it and crave it all day, and when you get home, it is time to binge. If you sneak in a drink the next morning, you just may put off withdrawal until you can drink again, but if not, you are in for the shakes, sweats, diarrhea, flu-like symptoms, fatigue, and much more.

And so the cycle continues, and every time you try to quit, the withdrawal gets worse and worse.

4. Ignoring Health Problems

You have likely heard that addiction "rewires" the brain. Know that the key issue here involves judgment.

It is like converting your car to run on a different kind of fuel. This fuel is harmful to the vehicle in the long run, but very hard to switch off once you begin using it because it is all the car will accept now.

A byproduct of this fixation on alcohol is that creepy voice inside your head that whispers bad ideas to your conscious:

Do not worry about (health issue x), you are fine. Just drink more water and eat something.

It is not because of the drinking, it is because I need to work out more and eat better.

The addicted brain will try to reason its way around the fact that alcoholism is directly causing health problems.

5. Mood Impairments

As mentioned, alcohol is a depressant. This is one reason why it is so attractive to people who work in high-stress environments such as law enforcement officers, to name one profession.

Remember our talk about hyperarousal? Whether it is PTSD or general anxiety, many of us spend far too much time in this amped-up state.

Now, do not take this the wrong way, because alcohol is absolutely not the answer, *but* I cannot truthfully say that it does not temporarily alleviate the effects of prolonged hyperarousal.

As a depressant, alcohol helps to bring you down from this "fight or flight" state. It helps you to feel more relaxed and less high-strung.

The problem, of course, is that alcoholics do not just say, "Well, those two drinks took the edge off, so I am done for the night." They drink another, and another, and another, until they have overshot the mark by a country mile or two.

This is when the parts of the brain that give us sadness, anxiety, anger, and self-esteem issues start taking over.

Sound familiar? As in, does it sound like a direct route to depression? It is.

In the interest of reaching as many of you in law enforcement as I can, I want to expand this field to accommodate anyone who has become addicted to other substances as well.

Remember from the introduction: Even if it seems counter-intuitive, the rate of alcohol *and* substance addiction in police officers is disproportionately higher than the rest of the population.

To be clear, I am referring to any potentially addictive substance, both legal and illegal, that law enforcement officers and the general public have statistically evidenced problems with, including:

- Opiates

- Nicotine

- Cocaine

- Heroin (number one)

- Meth

In many ways, your brain follows similar behavior patterns with each substance, alcohol included. For example, the impairment in your judgment that causes you to ignore health problems caused by alcohol addiction, for example, is prevalent among opiate, tobacco, and other addictions as well.

As such, I will make sure to include some of the symptoms unique to hard drug/opiate abusers in the following breakdown so you can have a more complete picture.

1. Using Alone

Sure, some alcoholics will see fit to drink alone, but generally, alcohol is more of a social drug. In fairness, this can be attributed to being legal and socially accepted to a degree. Still, people are more likely to abuse hard drugs or opiates alone.

Hopefully, this raises a red flag in your mind, having learned what you have learned about the contributors to depression and suicidal ideation. Namely, withdrawing from social situations.

So, you are craving this substance that alters your judgment and, in many cases, inhibits your ability to identify bad decisions, and you are taking this drug alone. That is two strikes already.

2. Obsessing Over the Stash

Fearing withdrawal, the addicted brain wants to ensure that there is more than enough of the substance at all times. This is probably not news to someone in law enforcement, especially if you deal with drug abusers a lot – they always maintain a stash when they can.

I am considering this a "symptom" of substance abuse because it is centered around obsessive mentalities, and because it causes addicts to engage in illegal or dangerous behaviors to acquire more of the substance.

This leads me to our next symptom, making financial (or other) sacrifices.

3. Making Financial Sacrifices

As an addict's addictive tendencies grow stronger, they will become more and more obsessed with ensuring a steady supply and a full reserve. Oftentimes, this means dipping into their finances.

This is especially problematic when the addict's income is usually used to help support a family. The addiction causes money problems, the money problems lead to spousal arguments, the marital disputes can lead to a series of other issues.

4. Respiratory Diseases and Cancer

I am referring to smoking as the mode of ingestion here. Whether it is something that will kill you slowly (cigarettes) or something that will kill you quickly (crack cocaine), smoking anything is never a good idea.

And the problem is, a lot of people love smoking so very much, and they are so reluctant to admit that it is fundamentally unhealthy for you that they have supposedly innovated around the dangers with vaping.

They can use all the marketing ploys they want – e-cig manufacturers have not totally eliminated the dangers of smoking. The sources say that long-term safety is still questionable, given the use of propylene glycol and other potentially harmful substances used in e-cigarettes.

Ironically, these substances are correlated to the same issues that cigarettes are: lung disease, chronic obstructive pulmonary disease (COPD), and all the other unpleasantness.

It is just not a viable way of consuming something, drug, or not.

1. Greater Suicide Risk

This list definitely is not exhaustive; there are still many issues that drug use has a hand in, like immunosuppression, sleep problems, mood regulation, and so forth.

Let us conclude this list of symptoms with the strong correlation between drugs and suicide. According to AddictionCenter.com, more than 90 percent of people who end up committing suicide have experienced depression, substance abuse, or both.

The vicious cycle runs both ways: drugs leading to depression or depression, leading to drugs. In the first scenario, someone may start taking drugs socially or experimentally. After they become addicted, they enter a depressed mindset. They withdraw from society, destroy their relationships, and so on and so forth.

In the other scenario, someone already experiencing depression may use drugs for the dissociative effects they provide – allowing them to escape their reality in favor of a much more forgiving one. This causes the same problems as the above, adding in a little impulsivity and impaired judgment, and there is your recipe for suicide risk.

Speaking of, I want to bring this chapter to a close by directly listing the risk factors associated with suicide. So far, we have illuminated the issue in terms of how certain habits and thought patterns can enhance "suicide risk," but what exactly does that look like?

According to SAVE, Suicide Awareness Voices of Education, the warning signs of suicide (as quoted directly from their website) are:

- Talking about wanting to die or kill oneself

- Looking for a way to kill oneself

- Talking about feeling hopeless or having no purpose

- Talking about feeling trapped or being in unbearable pain

- Talking about being a burden to others

- Increasing the use of alcohol or drugs

- Acting anxious, agitated, or reckless

- Sleeping too little or too much

How do law enforcement professionals get to this place? Even without the series of poor judgment calls involving substance abuse, Jenna Hilliard of the Addiction Center describes that the consistent "exposure to devastation, life-threatening situations, and the physical strain of working long hours can lead officers feeling hopeless and anxious."

In wrapping up this chapter, I want to give you a quick snapshot of one of the most effective treatments that I will mention later in this book. Consider it a glimmer of hope, and a non-pharmaceutical one at that.

American psychiatrist and University of Pennsylvania professor Aaron T. Beck has dug some pretty serious inroads to effective suicide prevention using a cognitive therapy approach.

Long story short, Dr. Beck found in a landmark study that suicidal ideation and tendencies are different for each person and each mental health disorder, so a customized approach will often be better than prescribed antidepressants.

Beck believed that suicide occurs not just as a product of unbearable stressors, but as a result of *cognitive disturbances,* meaning mechanical problems in the way that the suicidal person receives and processes information.

Beck showed the world that, even though suicide surprises us in almost every case, we do not have to treat it like a mystery anymore. There are tangible indicators and practical means of identifying and addressing those indicators.

In that spirit, I would like to introduce the idea of self-directed treatment, which is the topic of our next chapter. Let me be very clear: The following strategies are **not** meant to replace the psychiatric treatments you will see in the following chapter. They are meant as a way to supplement these treatments, and/or as a first line of defense before you decide to pursue the treatment you need.

CTA 4:

Ask yourself if you should consider seeking assistance for mental health. Ask your loved ones and friends if they have seen any changes in you since you put on the uniform. It takes guts, but you're brave enough.

Chapter V: Strategies for Sustainability

Alright, so this is going to read like a massively long checklist, but do not worry – I have organized it.

This is how I want you to think of this chapter: Consider it your miniature handbook for the practical, day-to-day changes you can make in real life to keep your thought patterns in a positive place.

Law enforcement officers have to contend with more than just bad guys and paperwork. You have some pretty profound logistical hurdles to manage throughout the day, such as trying to communicate with tons of people and collect/organize information while in a car, on the phone, or out in the field.

Thankfully, I have been there. I know exactly what you are going through because I went through it too. That is why this set of strategies is perfect for your situation. Ready to make some changes? Let us take a look.

Take Charge of Your Day

Okay, I realize this sounds generically peppy, like something you would find on the back of a cereal box, but it is an invaluable lesson nonetheless. Here is what I mean by taking charge of your day: Instead of letting your morning push you through a quick-and-dirty routine using the threat of being late, you should already be a lap ahead.

Let us say, like a lot of us, your normal routine is to wake up as late as possible, hastily brush your teeth and throw on the uniform, grab some coffee, watch your kids (if you have them) eat breakfast, kiss the spouse and then head out.

You have not had time during this whirlwind of a routine to consciously reflect on the fact that there is a chance, albeit a relatively small one, that you will not come home. You have not had a chance to give thanks for what you have. Already, you have denied yourself a couple of opportunities to face your stressors head-on. You are letting them sneak around in the back of your mind, which is where they do the most damage.

"Well, jeez, now that you have trashed my morning routine, what is your great idea, Mr. Enlightened?"

Okay, I deserved that. I understand it can feel a little bit invasive, me digging into your personal habits and all, but it is out of care and respect, so do not forget that.

Here is what I suggest: prime yourself mentally for the day ahead. Wake up earlier so that you can enter the proper mindset. Do not simply start your day with that "Crap, I'm gonna be late" feeling because you are steeping yourself in stress even before the uniform is on!

When you are in control, you are the one who dictates your routine by waking up early and giving yourself time. You have already struck a severe blow to your stress. So, what do you do with this time to get into the mindset? It is not rocket science. Here we go.

Meditation

Yes, meditation. I know, I know – I was not so hot on it at first either. It seems like the kind of "hippy-dippy" nonsense that I would have a laugh with my fellow officers about. We are supposed to be too tough for meditation, right?

But I want to explain something about meditation that may help to disarm your criticism right off the bat. First and foremost, you already do it to a degree. There are at least *meditative activities* that we all enjoy in one form or another, especially after a long workday.

For example, sitting there and staring at a wall for five minutes while you have that after-work snack. Going fishing on the weekends. Going on a run and just spacing out mentally for twenty minutes. Standing there in the shower and focusing on the sound of the droplets bouncing off your gourd as you take a much-needed mental break.

So you see, "meditation" is not this made-up trend. It is not some magical skill that you learn. Your ability to meditate is built-in. Consciously making an effort to meditate regularly, simply enhances your ability to enter that state.

Why do this? Because it confers a lot of essential benefits, both mentally and physically. Do not believe me? Check out this breakdown from Dr. Mathew Thorpe, who describes how meditation helps to:

- Relieve stress

- Fight depression

- Fight addiction

- Improve sleep

Uh, sound a tiny bit relevant to the issue of suicide risk among law enforcement, does it? It certainly should, because every single point on that list is correlated with suicide risk. What is more, meditation will sharpen your focus and allow you to better chase your aspirations.

Hopefully, it makes more sense now why Oprah Winfrey, Joe Rogan, Clint Eastwood, and other highly accomplished people take advantage of meditation.

Alright, alright, you might be thinking, but how? I do not know how to meditate. Oh, sure you do – we just need to focus on it, like I mentioned before.

There are different forms of meditation with different objectives. However, for beginners, I like to recommend what is called "breath awareness meditation" because it is very simple and just as effective as the other forms.

Sit on something comfortable or lie down. Close your eyes. Slow down your breathing and make each breath deeper.

That is the prep, now for the execution. There is only one step: just focus on your breathing. That is it. Do not think about anything else. If it helps, you can count your breaths.

Five minutes is an okay minimum threshold, and trust me, it will feel like forever the first couple times, but I like to shoot for closer to ten or fifteen. Still, we are not talking about waking up three hours early, so that is nice.

Of course, that hamster wheel of a mind is going to run off rather quickly – especially when you are a newbie at this. Do not be frustrated or discouraged. Simply return your focus to your breaths and resume.

After a few sessions, or maybe even one, you will notice that you have more patience and that you appreciate the little wins throughout your day more. You will spend less time fretting about unimportant crap and more time entertaining creative, substantive, and positive thought processes.

Meditation is awesome. Make fun of it if you want, but as someone who "drank the Kool-Aid," I can tell you that it is absolutely life-altering in the best way.

Alright, so you are sold on that, and you are definitely going to do it, right? Great. If you really want to multiply the benefits of meditation and start your day off in control, it is time to get physical. No! Not the song!

Exercise

I would feel so stressed out if I did not exercise. Not just because I would lack the stress-fighting benefits provided by exercise, but because I would be sick of everyone telling me to. Honestly, it is a broken record for a reason, especially nowadays – it is absolutely essential.

Unfortunately, recent workout trends have conflated fitness with swollenness. Everyone is so obsessed with deadlifting and benching now that they seem to miss the entire point of the exercise, which is to become healthier.

I will never forget what the jaded veterans on the force told me after I started. "Give it ten years in this job, and your waistline will expand." Well, it has been a solid 12 years, and I am a size smaller. I am in better shape than when I started, and I feel a lot better in uniform.

If you are already in shape, then great! Keep up the excellent work; I do not have to tell you just how helpful exercise really is.

However, if you are not working out, then it is time to "read and heed." Look, you do not have to be Mr. or Ms. Olympia, but you must absolutely do something – not just for your physical health, but for your mental health as well.

I do not mean to disparage weights, by the way. Weight training is an excellent form of exercise, one that I partake in regularly myself. It increases bone density and fortifies our joints against the strain of sitting for too long, sprinting after bad guys, and carrying that equipment around.

Nevertheless, by all means, please, no matter what you do, do not neglect the cardio. It is usually second fiddle to weights in terms of preference, I understand, but nobody says you have to make it the absolute worst for yourself. Prefer hitting stuff? Why not get yourself a heavy bag and some gloves? Hate running? Maybe you are more of a stationary bike kind of person. You do not have to be a top-performing athlete. Just do something and keep it consistent.

I am not trying to "scare you straight" here. Just to add even more relevance to the equation, working out with cardio exercises could literally be the difference between you being seriously harmed or not, on the job. If you end up in a fight with somebody who wants to hurt you, the last thing you want to do is gas out and end up completely vulnerable. You do not need to be Dwayne Johnson, but you definitely do not want to be the "no cardio" guy or girl. Those glamor muscles are meant for show, not survivability!

If you are not sure where to start, you do not need to fall down the trendy supplements and workouts rabbit hole. It does not have to be sexy and new. The old stuff still works.

Look, I can give you a sample 40-minute workout right now.

- 15 minutes of jogging, cycling, walking or other cardio (start light, get to at least 60 percent max HR, then maintain)

- 8 minutes of core strengthening (side bends/twists, crunches, weighted marches, etc.)

- 15-20 minutes of weight training (way too much to list, but rotate muscle groups on different days!)

Boom. You are done. You can move on with your day. No "keto cycling" or fricking "ab blaster" workout videos required.

So, why exactly am I recommending this so strongly, besides making sure you are not physically overpowered on the job? What does this have to do with decreasing suicide risk among the law enforcement community?

I want to bring your attention to the striking connection between exercise and suicide risk, as presented by a study in _Suicide & Life-Threatening Behavior._

The referenced study, which used depressed and PTSD-suffering veterans as its participant base, broke new ground in the connection between suicide and exercise by correlating the two _directly_.

Until now, it has been unanimously agreed upon that exercise helps to moderate the effects of depression. It helps with sleep patterns and negative thought patterns by releasing endorphins and other helpful agents in the brain.

By addressing the negative symptoms associated with depression, of course, you are indirectly combating suicide risk, since suicide and depression are closely related. Nothing too mind-blowing there.

However, this study actually proves a _direct_ link between exercise and suicide risk, though this connection still leaves much to be explored. Either way, the association is there, and I am all for it. Why? Because you can exercise almost anywhere. You can even do isometrics and mini-workouts throughout your workday. It is free, side-effect free, and natural.

Seriously. There is no good excuse not to exercise.

Remember Reading? I Remember Reading

The more bite-sized each morsel of digital media we gobble up becomes, the trickier it is for books to grab our attention and hold it like they used to.

Seriously. Take a look around. Everything has been truncated and chopped up so that we can fit five hundred pieces of information where there used to be a dozen or two.

You have got five-word memes dominating your social media feed, or at most, a post/status of a sentence or two. When news breaks, all the major outlets scramble to provide their two-paragraph info dump. Phone conversations have been usurped by shorter texts.

I am even guilty of pandering to the dying attention span. You think I enjoy packaging each distinct thought into a two- to four-line paragraph? Confession: I do not. The gift of gab, as it seems, is sometimes just as much a curse.

But hey, at least you are still reading a book. That is what I mean, by the way, when ordering you to read. Not a post. Not an article. But a book – at least twenty pages a day.

When you read, primarily upon starting your day, you help to actually attract positive energy. In the words of the venerable motivational speaker Les Brown: "What you expose your mind to first thing in the morning shapes how the rest of your day – and by extension, your life – will go."

This, of course, requires you to read material that is inspirational, motivational, and constructive. It does not mean that you have to gorge yourself on self-help books, though I am a big fan of the genre. Simply exposing yourself to an uplifting story of some kind is enough to provide a ton of mental health benefits.

What does this do to your overall mindset? It allows you to better adapt to tense and unpredictable situations by exploring alternative solutions instead of merely retrying the methods that keep failing. Mental flexibility, get it?

As police officers, I cannot think of a more helpful skill. I also appreciate the value of this flexibility in terms of depression, PTSD, and anxiety. The more adaptable you are to stressors, the less convincing their effects will be.

Next, reading helps your brain to communicate with itself and with the body better. This ringing a bell yet? Since depression especially is often measured by alterations in our neurochemical processes, such as the way the brain communicates and executes functions, it is safe to say that exercising this system is a great defense.

Ego Check #2: Yoga

You thought I was done prodding that tough and stoic exterior after meditation, right? Rest assured, I will do everything I can to humanize officers, which includes dismantling this idea of the "tough guy" or "tough girl."

If I can actually help to combat your depression, PTSD, and/or anxiety at the same time, then you better believe I am throwing it in this book. And that is precisely what is happening with yoga.

Look, I want to approach this thing from a Western medicine perspective if I may. I am well aware that you or one of your colleagues may be from an Asian country, and I absolutely respect the tradition behind the Eastern healing arts.

Here, though, we are all about the measurable, scientific expression of evidence. Do not tell me, demonstrate. Prove it. "Show me the money." You get the point. For that reason, I am going to explain Yoga less in terms of chakra alignment and more in terms of flexibility, blood pressure, mental health improvements, etc.

The American Osteopathic Association states that yoga is useful in promoting the body's ability to self-heal, which should always be prioritized over pharmaceutical intervention.

How does yoga accomplish this, you ask? It is easiest to break this down into both physical and mental benefits. The physical benefits include improved flexibility, strength, lung capacity, metabolism, weight loss, cardiac health, and much more.

The mental health benefits of yoga are even more potent as they help to prevent a myriad of stress- and inflammation-related diseases, including but not limited to heart disease, cancer, stroke.

Ok, now we have come to a point in which my wife is going to explain yoga in more detail since she was certified in yoga teacher training:

Unlike most other exercises and wellness routines – at its foundation, yoga - dedicates itself to awareness of your breath. Breath awareness is critical on many levels. First, focusing on your breath centers your brain's "monkey mind" - that endless chatter, you just cannot seem to shut up. If you aggregate and summon up all of your awareness to one event happening inside your body (i.e., breathing), it is pretty hard to focus on anything else.

Second, there are two types of nervous responses that happen in our body: fight or flight. These responses have been deeply ingrained over thousands of years of running from dangerous animals or dealing with enemy tribes. Whether it is fight or flight, your body quickly shunts blood away from your digestive system (and other areas) and towards the muscles of your extremities. This is what allows us to run as fast as we can or fight for our lives.

Right now, right where you are, take in a long, deep, slow breath in and relax on the exhale. How did that feel? Pretty darn good, right? Well, the physiological response that you felt is the other, calmer side to that nervous system response coin: the parasympathetic system. This is your "rest and digest" system.

The parasympathetic nervous system tells your body when it is time to relax for bed, following the circadian rhythm of sunrise and sunset. You can (and should) tap into this system anytime you need to, through this breathing technique.

So, you do not think this is all witchcraft, I will explain what happens here in terms of anatomy and physiology. In your body, there is a long, central nerve that runs from the base of your brain to your gut called the vagus nerve. You can think of this as a superhighway that provides a fast lane from brain to stomach.

Where do you think we get the phrase "gut feeling"? In order to send signals to your gut that you are not being chased by a lion (someone just stole your parking space), a deep breath stimulates this nerve. It sends signals to your gut to keep the blood there and stop sending it to your extremities. This is why they say, "No breath, no yoga. Know breath, know yoga."

Now, please allow me to share a bit of my own story with yoga to put your mind at ease. Full disclosure: I was **bored** in class. Everyone seems so serious and methodical, and those long gaps between the instructor's cues left me feeling bored and uninspired.

But then, I quieted my mind. I tried a little patience, and you know what? After just a couple sessions, I felt terrific. As a fan of fast-paced activity and just general goofing around, however, I still felt that I could find a better fit.

Lo and behold, I dug around a bit and found Sean Vigue. This guy has actually trained army units on army bases, and he has a hilarious personality. He was just what I needed to liven my routine up a bit, and if you are like me, I think you will enjoy his videos.

Type in SeanVigueFitness on YouTube, and there will be over 900 videos for you to choose from! Whether you are a beginner or intermediate, he has it all for you!

You can also visit his website: www.seanviguefitness.com.

Anyway, back to the awesomeness of yoga. In a nutshell, yoga is instrumental in alleviating stress, increasing focus and mental clarity, and preparing the mind for future stressors. Once again, I ask you:

Does it sound just a tiny bit relevant for law enforcement officers? Especially those battling depression, PTSD, and/or anxiety disorders?

It is time to abandon the silly stigmas and machismo-driven taboos. Let them laugh if they want. You know what you are about, and how important it is for you to be mentally healthy. Besides, in ten years, the haters are going to age twenty, but you will only age five.

Electronics

There are several ways in which our unchecked use of electronics can harm mental health. In some cases, it is the impact on our physical wellbeing that translates into increased risk for depressive disorders – remember the mind-body connection.

In other cases, the media we consume, how we consume it, and just how much of it some of us consume can have direct and negative impacts on our psychological makeup. It is an overused phrase, but this is yet another one of those things that can "rewire your brain" for the worse.

So, let us take it step-by-step here in terms of how screen time affects your mental health. First things first, let us talk about melatonin.

I have mentioned briefly that staring at a screen can mess up your brain's production of sleep chemicals. Phones nowadays use what they call "blue light" to illuminate their screens, which is responsible for this effect.

This is why the experts specifically recommend that you cut out the nighttime use of technology before anything else because the blue light impedes your body's ability to distribute melatonin.

Less melatonin means disturbed sleep, and we have already covered the indirect correlation between sleep, depression, and suicide risk. You need your sleep! Leave at least half an hour of screenless time before bed, say the experts.

Next, there is the whole dopamine loop fiasco. When you first wake up, what is the first thing you do? For many of us, the answer is to look at our phones. It does not help that most of us use our phones for alarm clocks.

So, after clumsily whacking your screen a few times and eventually deactivating your alarm, by not putting the phone down, you have already plunged your brain into the dopamine loop.

The dopamine loop is a lose-lose scenario. If you wake up to a few notifications, then you get that first shot early. About 4.9 seconds later, you are already feeling "strung out," and your breakfast with the kids becomes a backtrack to your neurotic phone-checking.

If you do not wake up to any notifications, that dopamine deficit implants some nasty thoughts in your head.

I am a loser. Nobody cares about me.

Even though you may not consciously voice these concerns, they are lurking in the background. And if you thought you were strung out in the first scenario; it is even worse when you wake up to no notifications.

The solution? I bet you can guess it. Just do not check your phone first thing in the morning. You already know what time it is, thanks to the peace-shattering alarm that pierced your consciousness.

Well, step one of the solutions to the dopamine loop is not checking your phone first thing in the morning. Step two involves doing something productive and self-directed, which is why this portion of the chapter comes after reading, exercise, meditation, and yoga. Hint hint!

Take a solid 30 at the very least. Get a grip on your morning, then check your phone.

So, we have mastered the first and last half hour of the day when it comes to countering the effects of electronics. Now for the next fifteen hours. For sanity's sake, we will group them all into the "when you are at work" category.

I want to present this idea to you in a way that does not compromise your vital work communications. I understand more than anybody that sometimes, you need to answer that work-related text, call or email quickly, but that does not mean you cannot take measures for your sanity.

What I mean is, instead of allowing yourself to be controlled by the constant dinging and buzzing of notifications, *you* be the one in control by checking them when you have time.

Yes, it is just as harmful to check your laptop and phone every 7 seconds as it is to let those notifications bombard you, so find a balanced approach. If you absolutely must keep your ringer and/or text notification on, then I understand. But do not do it for every single device you have. Check your devices when you are ready, and when you are not prepared, do not worry about it. See what I mean by control?

Once you learn how to efficiently regulate your device/social media use, you will notice improvements in your concentration and mood. This is because you will not be in a dopamine loop (or at least not as deep into the loop), and your brain will be able to engage in higher thought patterns once more.

Positive (and Negative) People

Alright, so this is a big one for law enforcement professionals. Look, I am just as guilty as you are – from time to time anyway – but after putting just a tiny bit of effort into this strategy, I have noticed huge dividends.

I am talking about people, people. You have likely heard that the company you keep can influence your outlook on life. In the words of one of my favorite influencers, Ed Mylett, your "environ**mental**" situation can strongly affect not only how you think, but what you accomplish.

In fact, Forbes goes so far as to cite a statistical likelihood of high achievement for people who immerse themselves in positive and high-achieving circles.

So, whether it is a promotion or merely a desire to feel less gloomy and frustrated all the time, surrounding yourself with positive people will pave the way for both of these things.

I realize that, as an officer, you do not always have complete control of who you spend your time with. It is highly advisable, however, that you exercise the control you do have to the fullest extent so that you can rid yourself of negative influences.

Not going to name names here, but I think we all know what I am talking about. The officer who is always complaining. The officer who treats everyone like an op-ed column. Every department has one or sixteen.

Ever heard of "mirror neurons"? For example, when you smile at a baby, and it smiles back, even though it does not really understand what a smile is, mirror neurons are hard at work.

This same mechanism stays with us as we develop into adulthood, and it can heavily influence learning, perspective, and even health. Neuroscientists have successfully correlated mirror neuron function with workplace success.

What does this mean? It reinforces the idea that surrounding yourself with people who are not only positive, but *better* than you at the job (or at least certain parts of it) is highly beneficial.

So, let us walk through how exactly you can accomplish this. Step one of the process is to compile a list of all your current workplace relationships, or at least who is in your proximity for the majority of the day.

Step two, assess whether or not they are a positive influence on you. When you think of them, are you inspired to work as hard as they do and share their perspective on matters, or do you think, "Man, I hope I never get that bad"?

Step three is where the real change happens. Now, I realize that you cannot always control who you are around and for how long, but there is always some degree of control. You do not have to settle being taken hostage by someone's griping and moaning all day.

For example, the best-case scenario is to simply stop hanging around that person. Great. If you have to be around them, however, you can gradually de-condition them, so their rants and raves become less and less frequent.

Instead of sympathetically nodding and saying "whoa, that is messed up...whoa, that's messed up," which, of course, just feeds the fire; it is time to close the loop. There are two ways to do this.

You can go totally Pavlovian and just remove the "reward" with your sympathy, by simply not providing it. Let them speak to an empty room (or patrol car). Let their words bounce back to their own ears in hopes that they will gain a little self-awareness.

If that does not work, you can replace your enabling response with a healthier alternative in an attempt to steer the conversation in a positive direction. Instead of saying, "whoa, that's messed up," you can find the silver lining/positive aspect of the situation and emphasize that.

One of two things will happen here if you persist with this technique. Either the person clutches on to their negative perspective and rejects your positive interpretation of what happened, or they will see the light and gradually change their outlook over time.

So you see, just as you can be positively influenced by others around you, so can you turn a negative coworker into a positive person. I have a super, super important disclaimer for you, though! Consider this your mantra.

You are not a bad person for walking away. You are not a bad person for walking away.

If that negative nelly simply refuses to see the light, then shed them. You are not a quitter, or a jerk, or a negative person for walking away from someone who refuses to be positive. At that point, your own survival depends on it. It sounds dramatic, but it is true.

Alright, so you have several options in terms of replacing negative people with positive people, blocking out negative influence, and even turning a negative person into a positive one. This is all good and fine in terms of your surroundings, but what about inside that head of yours?

Self-Talk and Mindset

Forgive the psych assessment here, but I am going to write a word, and I want you to carefully assess and record the emotional response you have to that word.

Retirement.

Many on the force are conditioned, per the above section, by the people around to think of retirement as some kind of blissful reward where nothing bad happens.

This can make a rookie, especially paint his current situation in drab colors. Constantly dreaming about retirement is actually a form of negative self-talk when you appreciate the implications that it silently feeds your brain:

Wow, I have such a long way to go. I am never gonna get there!

Same crap, different day. How long until I retire again?

This may make for a rousing Monday morning joke among your fellow officers or a half-amusing bumper sticker, but really, it frames your entire career in a negative light.

When I first started, I posted a retirement countdown timer on my MySpace profile! What the heck was I thinking?

Look, I have got a bit of a news flash for you: when you get to retirement, you are still you. No magical genie is going to snap their fingers and turn you into a positive person. The sad irony of the situation is, if you spent all those years dreading each day that you were not retired, that negative mindset would carry over into your actual retirement.

This is just one example of the power of mindset on perspective, performance, and overall happiness. People can influence your mindset, and your mindset can actually impact your physical health via the mind-body connection. Even more relevantly, it can feed the thought patterns that lead to depression, PTSD, anxiety, and yes – suicide.

I am not saying this to be pessimistic, but cautious: If you feel that you have a healthy and positive outlook on your career, your relationships, etc., then be aware that you need to *actively maintain* that mindset that you worked hard to achieve.

As a law enforcement officer, negativity will come for you in various forms, and it will persist. Do not assume that your initially positive mindset is Fort Knox. It will eventually break down if you do not take advantage of the above methods for safeguarding it.

A Final Tip

I want to close this chapter with what initially may sound like a strange recommendation, but hear me out.

You know how I have hinted at several points throughout this book that our brains (and bodies) are very slow to evolve?

Society has quickly exploded, especially after the industrial and agricultural revolutions. There is a larger disconnect between what our instincts tell us to do versus what we actually do. This is where problems occur.

Your primitive drive still wants you to chase down a woolly mammoth and kill it. You should still be foraging for berries, living in huts, and so on and so forth.

This is, of course, a laughable prospect today. We dismiss such "savagery" as the old, slow, and inefficient way, and we have moved on. But nobody told our mental blueprint, or at least, it is taking far longer to adjust.

Instead of using the stars, sun, and moon to tell time, we just check our phones. Instead of running from wolves, we sit for most of the day. Believe it or not, our brains are actually getting *smaller.* Creepy, I know.

Anyway, the point I am trying to make here is that you should give your brain what it wants. Let a little "savagery" in your life but in a sensible manner. I am not saying you should fashion a spear and bring it to work in place of your gun.

When you get home and/or on weekends, put that damned phone away. Go outside and get some dirt on your face. Run around with your dog, or your kids, or just by yourself act like a maniac (it is your backyard!).

Go fishing, go on a walk, put on some gloves, and punch something. Just...do something. Do something engaging, physical, and primitive.

I am not going to hurl a volume of stats at you, reinforcing this school of thought, though I am sure they are there. I am telling you this because it has immensely changed my life for the better. It does not even have to be an outdoor activity, necessarily. Just do something that makes your brain and body feel tired in the best way.

To quickly recap before moving on to the next chapter, which is all about treatment options for the various disorders we have covered, we discussed the following strategies for sustaining a positive perspective throughout your career in law enforcement.

First, take charge of your day. Wake up earlier. Ditch the phone. Do something that *you* can control instead of allowing your day (i.e., your notifications/emails) to control you right off the bat. What exactly is that something?

Meditation, for starters. Drop the machismo and just try it, *then* make fun of me if it does not work. It is super easy to do, as long as you are patient enough to manage runaway trains of thought. Sit, close your eyes, focus on your breath, and think of nothing else.

Parallel to meditation is exercise, which releases all kinds of feel-good chemicals to help you start your day in a positive state.

Moreover, it combats the physical effects of stress and anxiety while preventing future health problems.

Next, read. Allow your mind to ponder situations. The only guideline here is to make sure that you choose an uplifting (or at least not completely miserable) story.

To complete our triangle of mind-body awesomeness, yoga is the perfect addition to meditation and/or exercise because it promotes calmness, positivity, and physical wellbeing, all at the same time.

Remember, if you think it is boring, Sean Vigue can fix that. Look him up on YouTube.

To help the calming benefits of Yoga travel even further, monitor your use of smart devices and electronics. In his book, "Eat That Frog," successful author, salesmen, and speaker Brian Tracy talks about how checking your email too frequently decreases work productivity. He recommends checking email at 11:00 AM and 3:00 PM. I can tell you first hand that this helps immensely in workflow and my own sanity.

Next, do not forget to take a look at your environment, specifically, the people in it, and make the necessary changes to surround yourself with positivity. This does not always mean walking away from certain people, but when it does, it is better to do it decisively then to stick around out of a misplaced sense of guilt.

Especially if you are newer to the force, remember to establish a healthy perspective, and monitor your self-talk. If you are always telling yourself, "Man, I have such a long way to go before I retire," you are already framing things in a negative light.

Finally, feed your caveman brain. It is not an insult – we are all still running on an old operating system. Do engaging, primitive, and satisfying things, like running around with your dog, throwing stuff at other stuff, and even yelling. You are not crazy; you are just listening to yourself.

And if you are really listening to yourself and/or others, you may come to the realization that you cannot do it all on your own, which is okay. As long as you get treatment!

In the next chapter, I have called on three different mental health professionals to contribute their field-tested insights about their specialties in terms of treating Law Enforcement Professionals.

The more you know, the more you can act on. The more you act on, the better you can feel. The better you feel, the better you can execute the duties of one of the most stressful job fields on this great planet.

CTA 5:

Think of people at work who bring down the mood. Try to lift them up, or keep a safe distance. Their negativity can affect you.

Chapter VI: From the Experts

In this chapter, you will read guest excerpts from three people who provide treatment in the area of mental health and well-being. I am thrilled that they took the time to inform you as to some methods of treatment that are available for you.

I will begin with someone whom I have known since high school.

Diane Lowder, Licensed Psychological Associate

My name is Diane Lowder, and I am a Licensed Psychological Associate practicing in North Carolina. Basically, this means that I am a master's-level psychologist who has been actively licensed for 11 years and working in the mental health field for 13 years.

I began my career in the field of forensic psychology, where I worked as a staff psychologist in the North Carolina Division of Prison system for approximately 7 years. More recently, I have worked for the last 6 years as a psychologist for a local managed care organization assisting individuals with severe mental illness with moving toward living and working independently in their communities.

While obtaining my master's degree at UNC-Wilmington, I studied and majored in both clinical and substance abuse psychology. It is through both professional and personal experiences that I feel optimistic that I am able to make recommendations and have a discussion regarding effective mental health treatment and strategies for those living in the community and for law enforcement officers.

It is my opinion that these options are helpful for all individuals from all walks of life, but particularly for law enforcement officers; we simply must explore the options and find the right choice for each person based on what individual needs they may have.

When someone mentions the phrase "mental health," it's easy for one to create that negative stigma in their minds regarding what they "think" it means, i.e., to have a problem or to receive treatment, when mental health issues are actually more common than most people realize. In fact, according to the National Alliance for Mental Illness (NAMI), 1 in 5 U.S. adults experience a mental illness during the course of their lives.

Most prevalent among these disorders are: major depression, anxiety, PTSD, and dual diagnoses (meaning co-occurring mental health and substance-related issues). It's also important to note that these disorders also co-occur across all genders, ages, cultures and ethnicities. Additionally, it should be noted that suicide is the 10th leading cause of death in the United States, the 2nd leading cause of death between ages 10-34, and has increased 31% overall since the year 2001.

One final statistic of note involves the delay between onset of mental illness and treatment, which is 11 years on average. These numbers are staggering alone, but that final number amazes me every time I see it. My hope is that with more education, the stigma surrounding mental illness will one day be obsolete.

There is an astounding variety of treatment types that one can receive with regard to mental illness, all based in various philosophies and backgrounds. One could write for days and publish endless volumes of books regarding these different treatment options (and many have).

I would encourage you to take this brief review on just a few of the most effective forms of treatments and explore them at your own leisure to find one that best suits your own personal needs.

The most common form of treatment that most people are familiar with is psychotherapy, aka "talk therapy." These types of therapy are successful because one is able to sit in a room with an absolute stranger and discuss the issues bothering the individual, with the objective of finding new coping mechanisms to resolve those issues.

This type of treatment is one of my "go to" options with regard to recommendations for those seeking help. The wonderful benefit of psychotherapy is the many varieties available, allowing each individual to choose what's best for them. There are cognitive therapies, behavioral therapies, cognitive-behavioral therapies, dialectical behavioral therapy, mindfulness therapies and EMDR, just to start. All of these therapies have been proven to benefit depression, anxiety, PTSD and substance use; therefore, I'd like to briefly discuss each of these.

Cognitive therapy operates with the idea that our thoughts affect our emotions; therefore, our negative thoughts or self-talk can significantly impact our depression or anxiety, which ultimately impacts how we function in our personal lives.

Cognitive therapy helps an individual identify those negative thoughts or "cognitive distortions" and create new, more positive ways to cope with one's issues. This form of therapy is generally short-term and goal-directed. The individual and therapist create a treatment plan with specific goals to achieve during treatment, assigning "homework" between sessions for the person in treatment.

Behavioral therapies are focused on specifically changing certain problem behaviors that are identified by the person seeking treatment. You've heard of Pavlov's dogs? While different, this treatment method is similar in that the person seeking treatment learns new behaviors and "trains" themselves to change the "old" behaviors.

Some specific types of behavioral therapy treatments are: aversion therapy (pairing unhealthy behaviors with negative outcomes. For example, the unhealthy coping mechanism of alcohol abuse is like pairing substance use with becoming physically ill) and systematic desensitization (where one identifies situations that provoke depression or anxiety and pair those with relaxation techniques. The goal being that after repeated "triggering" of the individual, the pair will no longer cause the stress and the person will remain calm).

Cognitive-behavioral therapies (CBT) combine the two previous therapies (cognitive and behavioral) into one of the most popular and widely used therapies for both anxiety and depression. This therapy focuses on addressing both the negative thoughts and the behavioral patterns that go along with the anxiety and/or depression mindset.

Once again, a person in this therapy learns to identify their cognitive distortions (negative thought processes), often through the use of journaling, or other "homework," and works with the therapist toward specific goals.

Additionally, once behaviors are identified, activities in sessions or "homework" can include practicing relaxation techniques or other newly learned/healthy coping skills. Similar to the other therapies, this form of treatment is also time-limited and goal-directed by the individual seeking treatment.

Dialectical behavioral therapy (DBT) is a form of cognitive-behavioral therapy that was originally made popular by its success in treatment with individuals with borderline personality disorder. In the years since it was developed, research has proven its benefit to other populations such as the substance use and depression communities.

The main goal of this form of therapy is to teach skills to cope with and regulate stress while improving relationships with others. DBT is a structured therapy that actually combines both individual and group therapy sessions. DBT is based on a philosophical concept of "dialectics" which supports that everything is based on opposites and that change occurs when one opposing force is greater than the other. Like the other forms of therapy discussed already, DBT is also time-limited and goal-directed therapy, but arguably more intensive given the individual and group therapy aspects of treatment.

Mindfulness-based therapy is based on the stress-reduction and cognitive therapy models. Many forms of therapy actually combine these practices, such as DBT and CBT. This form of therapy is particularly helpful in preventing relapse for individuals with chronic depression, and has been shown to assist with anxiety and addictions as well. The idea is to combine cognitive therapy with meditative practices.

It is also a time-limited and goal-directed therapy (8-weeks); however, this is group therapy. Sessions generally consist of *learning about meditation techniques and the relationships between the ways one thinks and feels (cognitive therapy components).*

Between sessions is actually where much of the work is completed in this form of treatment. An individual practices those mindfulness techniques in their own lives through "homework" involving guided meditations.

Eye movement desensitization resolution (EMDR) therapy is an interactive therapy used to relieve psychological stress. It is an extremely effective treatment for individuals who have experienced traumas and post-traumatic stress disorder (PTSD).

This form of therapy involves an 8-stage approach to treatment that requires recalling upsetting memories while engaging in side-to-side eye movement or other sensory input. Though controversial since its onset in the 1990s, research has shown that it has been arguably just as successful in treating PTSD and trauma as other trauma-focused cognitive behavioral therapies.

As noted above, there are many forms of psychotherapy treatments in addition to those noted in this article to which all sufferers of anxiety, PTSD and depression may choose to engage in. The discussions in this article are also extremely brief; I would therefore encourage you as a law enforcement officer to further explore these treatment options or others if you are interested in seeking help.

Never be afraid to ask questions or seek treatment. If you find that one form of therapy does not work for you, perhaps a different style or even therapist will.

- Diane Lowder

Next, you will learn from a certified life coach. When I asked Kelly if she could help me out, she did not hesitate, because she understands how stressful the job of law enforcement can be. She took it as a high honor to write for you, so I hope you heed her advice well.

I know that the title of "life coach" is not immune to stigma, but don't just dismiss this stuff as a meaningless fad right off the bat. People's lives have been changed with the help of their life coaches. Her excerpt begins below.

Kelly Mobeck, CPC, CEF, NLPP
Certified Performance Coach, Certified Facilitator/ Trainer, NLP Practitioner

When life-coaching first showed up in the personal development arena, it was presented somewhat vaguely and not really trusted. People could not discern whether it was a profession that was actually credible or just the latest "quick fix" or fad.

This started in the late 80s early 90s, and much work has been done to ensure the credibility of the profession of coaching so that people are creating value shifts, thereby achieving the outcomes they want in life.

Fast forward to today, and we have personal, professional, executive, business, health, and life coaching, just to name a few. And the profession is now widely acknowledged as a means for assisting people in making sustainable changes in both their personal and professional lives, often times rather quickly.

For the purpose of this book, and to illuminate the ability of coaching to assist police officers with the immense day-to-day stress and trauma associated with their jobs, let's focus on life coaching as a resource for providing work/life harmony and stress management.

First, I want to be really clear that coaches are not doctors or therapists. We are not licensed, and we are upfront and clear with our clients about this before beginning the coaching partnership.

We know our lane, and we stay in that lane with our clients. We will be sure to instruct our clients to follow all doctor and therapist orders. Also, when working with a coach, be sure they are certified by a reputable school so that you can trust they have been trained well.

I often recommend schools that have been acknowledged and approved by the ICF (International Coaching Federation), which is the governing board for coaches, because they have a strict code of conduct and ethics that we follow.

The key to coaching is dedicating all efforts to forward movement. This means focusing on the client's "agenda," which in this context would involve working through stress- and trauma-related mental health concerns.

The life coach partners with the client to identify the specific outcomes the client wants to achieve, after which both will create an action plan that outlines sustainable strategies for producing and maintaining those outcomes.

It is important to know that with anything you are creating, practice is required. You and your coach will co-create those practices, and your coach will hold you accountable to them as well as any other actions you declare to take. Coaching is a true partnership dedicated to creating the change you want in your life.

Creating the practice of consistently engaging in effective stress-management techniques can open you up to a whole new life - one that has you feeling in charge of your life vs constantly feeling at the mercy of your job's day-to-day stressors.

A coach will work with you to honor your inner desires, assess when you need to take breaks, and assist you with putting practices in place to take those breaks.

As police officers, you've probably already taken stress management courses, so a coach may not be teaching you anything new, or in some cases they might. However, your coach will introduce a higher level of accountability to your actions, guiding you to the harmony you want in your life through repetitive practice of those techniques until they become a natural part of you.

Your coach will be a committed accountability partner as you move forward so that your focus and practice create the results you want.

You and your coach will work to create a plan to take stress triggers out of your life, beyond your job, so that you are not adding to the stress you already have when you come home from work. We don't often stop to think about that, and it is important to look at the whole of your life to establish what is working and what is not working so that you are not adding to your daily stress.

A coach will work with you to establish a plan of action that will create the shifts necessary to maintain harmony and remove unnecessary triggers and habits that don't support your positive development.

A coach will also help you identify the forces in your life that are zapping your energy. With a coach, you'll be given the opportunity to assess these sometimes hidden issues and find solutions to them. Stress is often the root of many problems, so working with a coach can absolutely help you to relieve anger issues, unhealthy habits, insomnia, and impatience.

When stress is causing you to feel out of control, the coach will support you and remind you of what to do and assist you in your accountability with it. This kind of support will guide you to a happier and even more fulfilling life, while also dealing with the day-to-day stress of your job.

You don't have to be perfect to be happy. In fact, there really is no such thing as humans being perfect. A coach will assist you in the benefits of taking it easier on yourself and finding ways to acknowledge the contributions that you've made on a daily basis while releasing the work day.

Some coaches are certified as NLP (neuro-linguistic programming) practitioners, which is extremely helpful in dealing with trauma, and highly recommended. Coaches who are trained and certified in this method utilize NLP as a technique to assist clients in removing anchors and triggers that are not serving them, often from trauma, and assist them in building new anchors and strategies to support them moving forward.

If a coach is not trained in methods specific to trauma victims, they will refer you to someone who is and/or make a recommendation for specific trauma-related assistance with a therapist, doctor, etc.

There are many coaches out there who have had specific training in addressing trauma, so there are definitely resources for you in the area of dealing with and handling trauma in the coaching field.

Coaches, like police officers, share the same commitment to service, and at the end of the day, a coach wants you to thrive and let go of what potentially limits you while assisting you in being the best version of you. Thank you for your service.

- Kelly Mobeck

Now the next excerpt features Dr. Bobby Bodenhamer, and he specializes in Neuro Linguistic Programming. He and I teamed up to coauthor this section.

I first met Dr. Bodenhamer in 2006, after dealing with symptoms of PTSD from my deployments to Iraq when I was in the Marine Corps. Dr. Bodenhamer helped me immensely. Just like Diane and Kelly, he is honored to be writing for you.

Dr. Bob Bodenhamer, Neuro Linguistic Programming

The Power of Association and Dissociation in Healing PTSD

Its essence: How to greatly reduce, if not eliminate, PTSD

Exercise Introduction:

1. Think of a time when you were feeling a great deal of emotional pain, such as that following trauma. Form an image of the point of the trauma.

2. When you recall that time of pain, do you see yourself in the image? Do you see yourself in that image of the trauma?

3. If you **do not see yourself** in that traumatic event, how are you feeling? Does it not feel like you are re-experiencing that event?

4. Now, **mentally step out** of that image and see the younger you in that image. When you **see yourself** in that traumatic event, you are **outside of it**.

5. By seeing yourself in that memory, how much did the traumatic feeling decrease?

6. If you still feel some of the traumatic experience, just mentally move that image further and further away until it disappears over the horizon.

7. How does that change your feeling from the trauma?

Explanation of How Association and Dissociation Work:

How does one police officer come home from numerous dangerous shifts seemingly unscathed from all the crime and disturbing situations of police work, while another police officer who experienced the very same shifts comes home greatly affected? He/she will suffer flashbacks of the crime scene as if he were still there. Indeed, many of these PTSD (post-traumatic stress disorder) sufferers come home so damaged that they are unable to function as fathers and husbands. Regrettably, these officers often turn to drugs and/or alcohol to dull the pain of crime. Consequently, the rise of suicides among police officers is an alarming issue for all of us.

Modalities and Submodalities

Before moving to the substance of this paper, the reader needs to both know and, importantly, understand the basics of brain function. It is very simple. How does outside information get into the brain for processing? It comes primarily through our five-senses: pictures, sounds, feelings (tactile), smells and tastes. We refer to these five senses as modalities.

What information comes into the brain through our eyes will be stored and recalled as a **picture**. What comes into our brain through our ears will likewise be stored in the brain as a **sound**.

When it is recalled, it will be recalled as a sound. And, what comes into our body as a **feeling** will be recalled as a feeling.

Let's experiment:

Consider driving home from work to your suburban home. How do you know which driveway belongs to your house? Your brain unconsciously (out of awareness) has an image of what your house and driveway look like. When you get close enough to unconsciously see your driveway, your brain recognizes your driveway out of all the driveways that you have driven by. The process is like the brain calling out your name, "Joe, there is your house, turn in that driveway."

Recall what the house that is beside your house looks like. Note where you see your neighbor's house. How close to your eyes is it? Is it close to your eyes and your face or is it further away? Now, get a mental image of your house… how close is it to your face?

Not only does the brain learn via our five senses, it also has smaller components inside these. Since our focus is on the visual (picture) modality, I will share with you some submodalities of the visual "modality." The term "submodalities" is referring to the smaller parts of what we are seeing. For instance, some of your pictures will be in color while other pictures will be in black and white.

These submodalities have meaning. For instance, for most people a picture in color carries more importance than a black and white picture. Also, a picture that is seen closer to the face will have more significance than a picture seen far off. I'm sure you have heard someone say in reference to a problem that they have experienced, "It is no longer an issue with me, I have distanced myself from it." Brains are literal. When one distances himself from a problem, he unconsciously moves the image of his pain further and further away from himself.

Experiment:

Form an image of a traumatic experience - maybe a time when you saw a child who was a victim of a horrible crime. Or maybe you saw someone badly hurt at a crash scene. Notice how it feels.

117

Now, mentally **move that image further and further away.** As you move that image further and further away from your face, how does the feeling change? I know that this sounds strange, but you can do it.

The question:

What makes the difference? How can one come home from the end of a dangerous shift unscathed while another returns home experiencing mental turmoil? The one that comes back in mental turmoil is often given the label PTSD – post-traumatic stress disorder. Many of our police officers, military personnel, and other first responders are labeled this way. As a result, the individual ends up identifying with the label. He/she will do this by creating beliefs that identify the belief as "I am a PTSD."

In doing this, the person has solidified in his or her mind that PTSD is a "thing" that he or she has. They experience it as being "real" when it isn't. PTSD, as well as most if not all emotional issues, is not a "thing" that we have, like catching the flu. PTSD is the result of the brain's learning that some event resulted in a lot of pain, and is therefore something to be avoided.

How does the brain construct PTSD, etc.?

The brain constructs PTSD through the same processes that the brain learns anything – through the five senses. PTSD is the result of the brain's constructing pictures, sounds, feelings, smells and/or tastes about the event. This happens with PTSD as with any learning from a highly emotional experience. With PTSD, the learning occurs deep in the mind. It does this through the construction of new neural connections via the creation of many brain cells and thousands upon thousands of new synaptic connections.

Figure 1 – Synaptic Connection

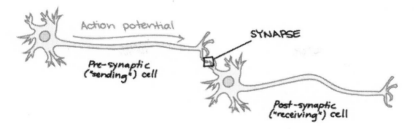

Synaptic connections are the way the brain connects one cell to another. Brain cells do not touch each other. There is a gap between cells, and it is through these gaps that new connections are made. **These gaps are called the synapses.** Communication between cells takes place using brain chemicals (neurotransmitters). By the way, drugs work by affecting the exchange of these chemicals.

The Submodalities of "Association" and "Dissociation"

How can one officer come back from a live-fire incident traumatized and suffering from PTSD, while another officer who was in the very same live-fire incident come back seemingly untouched? He experiences no signs of PTSD. He sees himself in the experience from his present context. He is no longer in the battle. He has moved from the battle to home.

A very important visual submodality in recalling traumatic experiences is whether you **do not see yourself (associated)** in the image in that past traumatic experience or whether you recall **it seeing yourself (dissociated) in the memory.** Let me explain:

1. **First:** we can recall a memory **"associated."** This means that we mentally place ourselves in that memory, seeing it through our own eyes, hearing the same sounds and feeling the very same as we did in the memory. You know that you are associated when you recall a memory and **you do not see yourself** in the memory. When associated, you are imagining yourself there in your body; thus, you are looking through the eyes of "then" and not the eyes of "now".

2. **Second:** *the second way that we can recall a memory is to recall it **"dissociated".** When recalling a dissociated memory, you see yourself in the memory. You are recalling that memory and **visually, you see yourself in that memory**. You see the younger you in the earlier memory. **Dissociating from a memory for most people greatly reduces the emotional intensity of that memory.** Likewise, associating yourself into a memory greatly intensifies the "feeling" that you receive from the memory.*

What happens when the officer is triggered back to the frightful experience of the bad fight, or a shooting, etc?

He mentally goes back to the traumatic experience and associates into that memory. He is telling his body that that event is happening all over again. There is no wonder that he experiences so many emotions. However, when the officer dissociates (steps outside of) the memory, essentially seeing himself on the battlefield from his present position of being safe at home, the intensity of that memory will be dramatically reduced.

*As an example, PTSD happens when the officer is triggered back to the frightful experience, like a scene involving numerous casualties. He mentally goes back there and associates into that memory when triggered. He is telling his body that that event is happening all over again. There is no wonder that he experiences so many emotions. However, when the **officer** dissociates from the memory by seeing himself at the scene(s) from his present position of being safe at home, the intensity of that memory will be dramatically reduced.*

Are you having difficulty experiencing "dissociation"?

To experience "dissociation", imagine yourself floating out of your body. That's right, just mentally "step outside" of your body, and if you wish, you can move all the way up to the top of the ceiling. With your back against the ceiling, see yourself and any other person below you.

If you are having difficulty doing this, sit in a chair and be very aware of yourself in the chair. You can feel the arm rest. Now, physically, step out of the chair and walk around to the back of the chair. Imagine seeing yourself sitting there in the chair. Reach out your arms and place your hands on top of your shoulders. While you are doing this, give yourself a massage sitting there in the chair.

Now, if you are still having a difficult time creating an image of yourself, then stand before a mirror. See yourself in the mirror, as you have done many times before. Now, seeing yourself in the mirror, close your eyes and picture yourself in the mirror. Just imagine yourself there in the mirror.

All of these are examples of "dissociation". We use it a great deal in doing NLP (neuro-linguistic programming) therapy. Dissociation, or stepping outside of yourself and imagining yourself anywhere you choose, tends to remove or greatly decrease emotional responses to memories.

If you see yourself in that memory, you are dissociated from that time, and are therefore less likely to feel the pain that you felt when you had the experience.

One of the major things that an NLP therapist does with someone suffering from PTSD is to get that officer to be present, and not reliving the trauma. Invariably, when an officer has a "flashback", he/she is immediately back inside that memory. They recall that memory associated (do not see themselves), and as such, their brain is telling their body that they are back at the scene(s) re-experiencing that trauma.

If you are suffering from PTSD or you know someone who is, then just "step outside" yourself when recalling the memory of that call. See that younger you there on scene and know that he has made it. **He is safe now.** He doesn't need to experience any more of those panic attacks. Just make sure that you and/or the PTSD is recalling all memories of pain from a dissociated position - you see yourself in that traumatic event, but you are not in it. You are home and totally not on the battlefield.

With a high number of PTSD sufferers, just visually dissociating them can bring about great positive change. This works on any traumatic event. And here is something else you can do: Once you "see yourself" there in that traumatic event, know that you can move that picture out way out in front of you and way away from you. Or, if you see it behind you, then send that image way, way back so that it has no more effect on you.

There are other things that you can do with this pattern. Go to www.renewingyourmind.com for more patterns. That is a Christian NLP site, so be aware. We have another website, www.masteringstuttering.com, that is full of NLP patterns. Don't be concerned if you aren't a stutterer. People who stutter are triggered to stutter primarily by having the "fear that they will stutter." Experiencing this fear almost guarantees stuttering.

Indeed, for many stutterers, the fear of stuttering and believing they will be made fun of is a traumatic experience for them. Sometime in their past, the stutterer was traumatized, and the stuttering started. On this website, you will find several patterns centered around trauma, fear and anxiety.

The internet has tons and tons of articles and techniques to help people take control of "running their own brain" rather than letting someone else or some emotion run their brain (see http://nlpuniversitypress.com/.)

Now, back to where we started - you can dissociate from your body and mentally go anywhere you want to. By the way, there are people who grew up in great trauma. Such children naturally learn how to dissociate - how to go somewhere where it is not so painful.

Now, when this is very severe, the child can develop into what is called Dissociative Identity Disorder. And, if the child is sexually abused and it happens continuously for many years, that child can become an adult suffering from Multiple Personality Disorder. The child creates imaginary representations of themselves and they "associate" into whichever person they need at that specific time.

Several years ago, when I was teaching NLP in the Adult Ed. Department of our local community college, a young lady joined our class. She was licensed as a Professional Counselor (LPC). However, this poor lady had been diagnosed with dissociative disorder, and she was placed on disability. Upon examining her, I soon discovered that she was imagining living her life as a small child on top of the refrigerator.

Her father was an alcoholic. He beat her mother. Hollering and fighting were a daily occurrence. My student would imagine herself as a small child on top of the refrigerator. She felt safe up there from all the arguing and fighting. There was one major problem: she remained on top of the refrigerator into adulthood. Therefore, she was correctly identified with the dissociative disorder diagnosis. **Get out of that traumatic experience. You don't live there anymore.**

Something to think about:

The following statistics come from the Centers for Disease Control and Prevention's National Death Index:

- 45,390 American adults died from suicide in 2017, including 6,139 U.S. Veterans. Findings in this report reflect the most current national data (available through 2017).

The following reported statistics come from Bluehelp.org:

- So far in 2020, approximately 33 Law Enforcement Officers have committed suicide
- 2019: 228
- 2018: 172
- 2017: 168

I'm not going to go any further. This is upsetting and tragic. You can see the increase.

According to National Alliance On Mental Illness:

- 1 out of every 4 Law Enforcement Officers has suicidal thoughts at some point in their lifetime
- The suicide rate is higher amongst law enforcement officers at smaller departments

Contributed by Dr. Bobby Bodenhamer

CTA 6:

Start utilizing at least one new strategy and/or treatment you read about in this book that will help you improve your mental well-being. The time to start is now.

Chapter VII: Policing is NOT Who You Are, It's What You Do!

The knee-jerk reaction of most officers is to resist this idea of not allowing your career to define you.

"What the heck, Scott? Policing is in my blood. I am blue thick and through!"

In this final chapter, however, I'm going to show you through my own life experiences just how damaging of a mentality that can actually be.

I'm also going to back this advice up with some wisdom passed down by a number of influencers whom I have come to know as personal mentors (see the resources section). I encourage you to listen to what they have to say as well.

Police officers may be of the opinion that talk is cheap, and that words don't affect you, but the psychology of language can be a tricky little thing, and this is the perfect example.

Patrick: Hi there, my name's Patrick

Susan: Hi Patrick, what do you do for a living?

Patrick: Oh, I'm a police officer.

It sounds nitpicky, but did you catch that? Susan asked Patrick what he *does,* and Patrick told Susan what he *is.*

Most of us in the Western world define ourselves by our job titles. This kind of perspective is a blessing and a curse. It's a blessing because it allows us to ascribe our good deeds at work as personal virtues, and it's a curse because we hurt that much more when our work deals us more than we can handle.

You may like to think that your badge number is seared into your DNA, but it's not. Policing is what you do, not who you are. Acknowledging this disconnect doesn't mean that you're less dedicated than the other men and women in your department. It just means you have a healthier perspective.

Why healthier, you ask? Well, if you allow your "work self" to just blend into your true self, then you're at greater risk for addictions, PTSD, depression, and other suicide-related issues because you lose your sense of self.

Instead of leaning on your personal values when things get tough, your feelings of self-worth and happiness are at the mercy of the chaos that occurs during your work day. When policing becomes who you are, you have internalized it in an unhealthy way.

That's the difference between maintaining a strong resolve and riding that roller coaster of thrills, frustrations, boredom, and so forth until a career-ending injury or retirement cuts it all short.

Then what do you have? If you spent decades operating like you are what you do, what happens when there's no more do? What are you?

Depressed. Addicted. Stressed out. Et cetera.

I'm not reading from a pamphlet here. I can relate to this personally. Just like our example above, when asked about my occupation, I would always say "I **am** a K9 officer."

Don't get me wrong, it was an achievement I'm very proud of, and I worked hard to make it happen. I spent ten years networking and learning about K9 police work before finally earning my spot in October of 2012 – dream come true!

But there it is again – the "I am." I was confusing my job with my being, and though it hadn't bit me yet, it was about to.

Reasonably so, family obligations after my first child (in 2015) forced my wife into a tougher position. She was bringing in the majority of the household income, maintaining the home, and often watching the little one by herself while I was out "being who I was," the K9 officer.

By the time February of '16 rolled around, she was over it. She told me it was time to quit the K9 unit and the force altogether.

She had had enough – nine years, to be precise – of my off-duty hours, my stressed demeanor, and all the extra work.

But quitting didn't feel like an option for me. Not because I was worried about getting another job, but because I felt like I *was* this job. The idea of quitting initially felt like becoming a different person altogether. It felt like I would lose my identity.

So I forced it along, of course. For nine cringeworthy months, I took off weekends and doubled my efforts at home. Still, I simply wasn't present enough. Not only physically, but mentally. I wasn't being the best husband and father I could be, and I didn't even know it.

Finally, come October of that same year, my wife told me she was considering life without me and she basically said it was either her or the job. This idea crushed me. It was a wake-up call to be sure. Not only was it disheartening that she felt that way, but I knew at that moment that I would have to leave the K9 unit.

 So, I said goodbye to my crazy and loyal K9 partner, Romac, and left. Why? Because, and please consider this a neon sign, policing is NEVER worth a marriage. Never. You won't work as a police officer your whole life, but you can choose to love someone and enjoy being with them as long as you shall live.

After being placed into a more family-friendly assignment, I experienced a bit of a flip-flop. My home life improved, but I felt completely dismantled as a person. This is when the anxiety, depression, and anger began to take hold. All because I thought I *was* a K9 officer.

I wasn't a K9 officer. It was simply the path I was following at that time, and the fact that I couldn't see that almost cost me my marriage. The nine months of turmoil I caused, believe it or not, was the lesser punishment for my unhealthy perspective.

Do I still miss it? YES. I always will, but I've learned that I can't dwell on the past. I'm not what I do. The job remains the job, and I will evolve into something else. That's the disconnect you need to appreciate, and don't let anyone tell you it's a "negative attitude."

This is how I want you to feel. If the job is too stressful for you and/or your family, recognize it. Don't justify it if it's deeply affecting you. Always remember that you can move onto something else and still retain your identity. You'll be leaving a job, not yourself.

Take professional athletes, for example. While they're racking up those amazing accolades, they're being adored by thousands of fans. After the lights turn off and everyone goes home, however, the mental battle can be surprisingly difficult. From high to low in five minutes, sometimes.

Before wrapping up with a few words of attempted wisdom, I just want to thank you for allowing me to share all of this with you. I'm here because I care about what happens to you, and I've been where you've been in one way or another.

Remember who you were before you became an officer, and you'll find who you will become after you're an officer. Love what you do, but don't confuse it for who you are. Help yourself but get help when you need it. Your mental health matters.

CTA 7:

** If you enjoyed this book, please give it a five-star review on Amazon.

** Subscribe to my YouTube channel: The 10 Code Mindset

References

Alcohol use disorder - Symptoms and causes. (2018). Retrieved
  31 March 2020, from https://www.mayoclinic.org/diseases-
  conditions/alcohol-use-disorder/symptoms-causes/syc-
  20369243

Benefits of Yoga. Retrieved 31 March 2020, from
  https://osteopathic.org/what-is-osteopathic-
  medicine/benefits-of-yoga/

COGNITIVE APPROACHES TO SUICIDE. (2001). Institute of
  Medicine (US) Committee on Pathophysiology and
  Prevention of Adolescent and Adult Suicide. Suicide
  Prevention and Intervention: Summary of a Workshop.
  Washington (DC) National Academies Press (US);.
  Retrieved 31 March 2020, from
  https://www.ncbi.nlm.nih.gov/books/NBK223847/

Corruble, E., Benyamina, A., Bayle, F., Falissard, B., & Hardy, P.
  (2003). Understanding impulsivity in severe depression? A
  psychometrical contribution. Progress In Neuro-
  Psychopharmacology And Biological Psychiatry, 27(5), 829-
  833. doi: 10.1016/s0278-5846(03)00115-5

Davidson, C., Babson, K., Bonn-Miller, M., Souter, T., & Vannoy,
  S. (2013). The Impact of Exercise on Suicide Risk:
  Examining Pathways through Depression, PTSD, and Sleep
  in an Inpatient Sample of Veterans. Suicide And Life-
  Threatening Behavior, 43(3), 279-289. doi:
  10.1111/sltb.12014

Davis, H. (2020). Police officer suicide rate more than doubles
  line-of-duty deaths in 2019, study shows. Retrieved 31
  March 2020, from https://www.foxnews.com/us/texas-police-
  officer-suicide-rate

Felman, A. (2018). What are the symptoms of addiction?.
  Retrieved 31 March 2020, from
  https://www.medicalnewstoday.com/articles/323459

Fletcher, J. (2019). Is vaping bad for you?. Retrieved 31 March 2020, from https://www.medicalnewstoday.com/articles/327374

Juergens, J. (2019). Addiction and Suicide. Retrieved 31 March 2020, from https://www.addictioncenter.com/addiction/addiction-and-suicide/

Julson, E. (2018). 11 Signs and Symptoms of Anxiety Disorders. Retrieved 31 March 2020, from https://www.healthline.com/nutrition/anxiety-disorder-symptoms

Karen. (2018). 167 AMERICAN POLICE OFFICERS DIED BY SUICIDE IN 2018 - Blue H.E.L.P. Retrieved 31 March 2020, from https://bluehelp.org/blog/158-american-police-officers-died-by-suicide-in-2018/

Kosslyn, S., & Rosenberg, R. (2004). Fundamentals of Psychology: The Brain, The Person, The World (2nd ed.). Allyn & Bacon.

Mylett, E. (2018). #MaxOut Your Life: Strategies for Becoming an Elite Performer. JETLAUNCH.

Olson, A., & Wasilewski, M. (2016). 4 principles cops can use to overcome negativity and negative thoughts. Retrieved 31 March 2020, from https://www.policeone.com/health-fitness/articles/4-principles-cops-can-use-to-overcome-negativity-and-negative-thoughts-egerjFDoPjThtDx8

Police and Addiction. (2018). Retrieved 31 March 2020, from https://www.psychologytoday.com/us/blog/sure-recovery/201803/police-and-addiction

Purbasari Horton, A. (2017). How To Make Your Actual Work As Addictive As Email. Retrieved 31 March 2020, from https://www.fastcompany.com/40418508/how-to-make-your-actual-work-as-addictive-as-email

Robbins, M. (2017). The 5 Second Rule: Transform your Life, Work, and Confidence with Everyday Courage. Savio Republic.

Romano, D. (2020). [TED TALK] How To Rewire Your Brain: Neuroscientist Dr. Joe Dispenza Explains The Incredible Science Behind Neuroplasticity. Retrieved 31 March 2020, from https://hypnosistrainingacademy.com/neuroscientist-dr-joe-dispenza-ted-talk/

Santos, R. (2018). Break Addiction to Negative Thoughts & Emotions Joe Dispenza. Retrieved 31 March 2020, from http://growthevents.org/break-the-addiction-to-negative-thoughts-and-emotions-dr-joe-dispenza/

Selhub, E. (2015). Nutritional psychiatry: Your brain on food. Retrieved 31 March 2020, from https://www.health.harvard.edu/blog/nutritional-psychiatry-your-brain-on-food-201511168626

Tracy, B. (2002). Eat That Frog!: 21 Great Ways to Stop Procrastinating and Get More Done in Less Time (1st ed.). San Francisco, CA: Berrett-Koehler Publishers.

Trauma on the Job: Post-Traumatic Stress Disorder in Law Enforcement Officers. (2016). Retrieved 31 March 2020, from https://www.lexipol.com/resources/blog/post-traumatic-stress-disorder-law-enforcement-officers/

Violanti, J. (2018). PTSD among Police Officers: Impact on Critical Decision Making. Retrieved 31 March 2020, from https://cops.usdoj.gov/html/dispatch/05-2018/PTSD.html

Wack, M. (2020). 15 Symptoms Of Depression And Anxiety. Retrieved 31 March 2020, from https://www.betterhelp.com/advice/depression/15-symptoms-of-depression-and-anxiety/?utm_source=AdWords&utm_medium=Search_PPC_c&utm_term=_b&utm_content=75597921965&network=g&placement=&target=&matchtype=b&utm_campaign=6459244691&ad_type=text&adposition=&gclid=Cj0KCQiAvc_xBRCYARIsAC5QT9kRFOdkY-L0n-

OCyAR4XMkQbm8_MbXuLVsJngu_QWHKoq2kF2wSUG0a
AoUKEALw_wcB

Warning Signs of Suicide. Retrieved 31 March 2020, from
https://save.org/about-suicide/warning-signs-risk-factors-
protective-factors/

What are the five major types of anxiety disorders? (2014).
Retrieved 31 March 2020, from
https://www.hhs.gov/answers/mental-health-and-substance-
abuse/what-are-the-five-major-types-of-anxiety-
disorders/index.html

What Is Depression? (2017). Retrieved 31 March 2020, from
https://www.psychiatry.org/patients-
families/depression/what-is-depression

Made in the USA
Columbia, SC
02 December 2024